PRAISE FOR *DOUGLAS-FIR*

"Arno and Fiedler have crafted an insightful and engaging paean to the Pacific Northwest's most important tree. This is a book for anyone who wants to understand not only the ecological story of Douglas-fir but also how these majestic trees shaped the economic story of Puget Sound and the entire region."

—David B. Williams, author, *Too High and Too Steep: Reshaping Seattle's Topography*

"Stephen Arno and Carl Fiedler's inviting text *Douglas Fir* is filled with information about the versatile, resilient conifer that 'from firewood to flumes, flagpoles to flooring, snowshoes to spars, and liquor to lumber [fills] needs or niches in the lives of everyday people.' . . . Featuring multiple illustrations, historical photographs, and a list of notable Douglas-firs to visit across the US and Canada, the book is a comprehensive look at the fascinating tree."

—*Foreword Reviews*

"This book is a gift to those of us who love trees. It reflects decades of observation and research by two dedicated scientists, but is far more than a simple botanical treatise about a dominant forest tree. The authors not only tell the story of Douglas-fir as a species but describe in fascinating detail how our human relationship with this iconic, 'truly extraordinary' tree has shaped our ecosystems, our history, our economy and our cultures in so many different ways. This affectionate yet rigorously documented book should be a must for any library specializing in environment, history or politics."

—Nancy J. Turner, ethnobotanist and distinguished professor emeritus, environmental studies, University of Victoria

"The Douglas-fir of North America is an outstanding tree in many respects. Its beauty, great size and age, and role as a keystone species have given it a central emotional, spiritual and ecological role in the celebrated old-growth forests of the Pacific Northwest. For over 6,000 years humans in western North America have had a close cultural relationship with this species, and today, it is widely planted on six continents and ranks as the most economically important softwood timber species in the world. Arno and Fiedler have captured the cultural and ecological diversity of this extraordinary tree in a detailed and engrossing study that weaves science, history, and insight into a memorable book that will be enjoyed by all who love the native forests of the West."

—Chris Earle, forest ecologist and founder of Conifers.org

DOUGLAS FIR
THE STORY OF THE WEST'S MOST
REMARKABLE TREE

STEPHEN F. ARNO AND CARL E. FIEDLER

MOUNTAINEERS
BOOKS

MOUNTAINEERS BOOKS is dedicated to the exploration, preservation, and enjoyment of outdoor and wilderness areas.

1001 SW Klickitat Way, Suite 201, Seattle, WA 98134
800-553-4453, www.mountaineersbooks.org

Printed in Canada
Distributed in the United Kingdom by Cordee, www.cordee.co.uk
23 22 21 20   1 2 3 4 5

Copyeditor: Mindy Seale Fitch
Design and layout: Jen Grable
Cartographer: Martha Bostwick
Illustrator: Zoe Keller, www.zoekeller.com
Cover design: Jen Grable
Cover illustration: Zoe Keller

Library of Congress Cataloging-in-Publication Data record is available at https://lccn.loc.gov/2020004770.

Mountaineers Books titles may be purchased for corporate, educational, or other promotional sales, and our authors are available for a wide range of events. For information on special discounts or booking an author, contact our customer service at 800-553-4453 or mbooks@mountaineersbooks.org.

♻ Printed on recycled, FSC-certified materials

ISBN (hardcover): 978-1-68051-199-4
ISBN (ebook): 978-1-68051-200-7

An independent nonprofit publisher since 1960

To Dr. Roland Rethke, who in the early 1960s chose to inspire me and other students at Olympic (Junior) College to learn about forest ecology when he could have joined the faculty of a major university
—Stephen Arno

To my brothers, David and Mark, and the many other friends whose help allowed me to continue working on this book despite my medical problems
—Carl Fiedler

CONTENTS

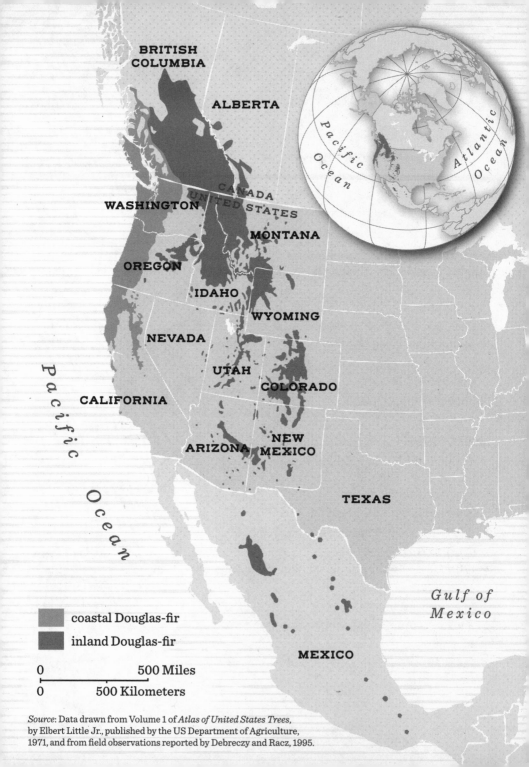

BRITISH
COLUMBIA

ALBERTA

*Pacific
Ocean*

*Atlantic
Ocean*

CANADA
UNITED STATES

WASHINGTON

MONTANA

OREGON

IDAHO

WYOMING

NEVADA

UTAH

COLORADO

CALIFORNIA

ARIZONA

NEW
MEXICO

TEXAS

*Pacific
Ocean*

*Gulf of
Mexico*

MEXICO

coastal Douglas-fir

inland Douglas-fir

0   500 Miles

0   500 Kilometers

Source: Data drawn from Volume 1 of *Atlas of United States Trees*, by Elbert Little Jr., published by the US Department of Agriculture, 1971, and from field observations reported by Debreczy and Racz, 1995.

INTRODUCTION:
Nature's All-Purpose Tree

Most westerners familiar with native forests probably think they know the Douglas-fir, which is after all one of our most common trees, indigenous to all the western states, western Canada, and the high mountains in Mexico.

However, few people realize the many forms and strategies Douglas-fir adopts to occupy more kinds of habitats than any other American tree. The species comprises two varieties—coastal Douglas-fir and inland, or Rocky Mountain, Douglas-fir—and includes the giants of the coastal forest, luxuriant conical trees in young stands, stout old sentinels along grassy ridges, and wind-sculpted dwarfs clinging to high mountain slopes. Douglas-fir occupies both damp habitats, such as ravines and north-facing slopes, and droughty ones, such as south-facing slopes, and nearly all sites between.

In moist environments, coastal Douglas-fir is a pioneer species— one that depends on fires, logging, and other major disturbances to create the open conditions that allow it to establish and avoid stifling competition from shade-tolerant species like western hemlock and Sitka spruce. These shade-tolerant species, unlike coastal Douglas-fir, can produce abundant saplings beneath the mature tree canopy and eventually form thickets of young trees that, without another disturbance, gradually replace aging Douglas-firs and take over the forest in perpetuity.

Douglas-fir also inhabits some of the hottest environments, such as sunbaked rocky islands in Washington's San Juan archipelago, and the coldest ones that any trees can tolerate, including subalpine forests along the Continental Divide in Montana and Wyoming.

Both coastal and inland Douglas-fir are exceptionally resilient and quick to colonize following disturbances such as wildfire, logging, land clearing, and even residential developments, where it may later appear as a beautiful volunteer in a suburban yard. In the drier, fire-dependent forests of the interior West, some people view inland Douglas-fir as a sort of uncontrollable noxious weed, even though human efforts to eliminate fire are largely responsible for its proliferation. In inhospitable environments, Douglas-fir alone forms the native forest whether there are disturbances or not, such as in the high semi-arid mountains of southwestern Montana and southeastern Idaho, where the inland variety is the only erect tree. To sum up its adaptability, Douglas-fir is nature's all-purpose tree.

Douglas-fir has proved valuable to humans as well, beginning with the many native peoples of North America who have lived among and used these trees for millennia. The species has long had a reputation for producing good lumber and firewood, and native people have used it in numerous other ways, such as for making tools and preparing medicines (see chapter 5).

Coastal Douglas-fir formed the foundation for early development and commerce by Euro-American settlers in the Pacific Northwest, where a few hundred sailing ships overloaded with Douglas-fir lumber were dispatched to distant ports each year in the mid and late nineteenth century (see chapter 4). Douglas-fir continues to yield more high-quality construction lumber than any other tree in the world, and because of its superior wood qualities, it has been cultivated for timber products on six of the seven continents.

Paradoxically, long after it became the world's premier construction lumber, the tree's botanical identity and common and scientific names remained in dispute because its cones and foliage were very different from any other known species at the time. And its common name continues to confound because, as described in chapter 1, Douglas-fir is actually not a true fir.

As a research forester for the US Forest Service, I (Stephen Arno) have worked and lived among a variety of native

Douglas-fir forests from the Pacific Coast to the east slope of the Rocky Mountains for more than half a century. Continually amazed at this species' ubiquity, resilience, and usefulness to humans, I wanted to present a comprehensive profile of this world-renowned but underappreciated tree. I have collaborated with Carl Fiedler on other forestry-related books and journal articles, greatly benefiting from his contributions, so I was delighted when he agreed to join me in writing the book you now hold.

I first became aware of Douglas-fir as a five-year-old living on Bainbridge Island, which is nestled in Puget Sound near Seattle, Washington. My first paying job was to carry slabs of thick Douglas-fir bark that drifted onto the beach up a tall wooden staircase to supply my mother with her favorite fuel for the kitchen stove. The slabs would break loose from old-growth logs banging against each other in booms (floating masses of saw logs encircled by a string of logs chained together end to end) that tugboats towed from place to place.

Douglas-fir was by far the most familiar tree of my childhood. Over a period of a few years in the mid to late 1940s, my whole family helped my father excavate a massive old-growth Douglas-fir stump that crowded our driveway. Dad used saltpeter to speed up rot, and laboriously dug out and then chopped and hand-sawed through the huge roots. Finally he managed to jack the stump loose. Next he hired a neighbor with a World War II surplus duck, a six-wheel-drive amphibious landing craft, to pull the monster out of its pit and drag it out of the way. It then served me and my friends as a 7-foot-tall jungle gym.

Later as an outdoorsy youngster, my stomping ground was on the nearby Kitsap Peninsula, on the west side of Puget Sound. The land had been scoured and compacted by an immense glacier during the last ice age, and as a result was largely covered with poor soils. Nevertheless, I observed in wonder that in most places, stumps from the original Douglas-fir forest, which had been logged a half century earlier, were commonly 4 feet or more in diameter.

Wherever the original forest had been spared, it was dominated by craggy-barked Douglas-firs 4 to 8 feet thick and commonly more than 200 feet tall. Logging and sawmills were the mainstay of the rural economy in western Washington, and I learned that the Puget Sound mills had once loaded sailing ships with Douglas-fir lumber bound for San Francisco and other port cities. I also learned that in 1871 my grandfather, then six years old, and his extended family had sailed stormy seas from San Francisco to Puget Sound on the return voyage of a lumber schooner. According to my aunt's historical account, grandpa was the only family member who didn't get seasick and was thus able to help the crew and his family with chores.

We moved to the outskirts of Bremerton on the Kitsap Peninsula in 1950. My parents bought a small house on about 120 feet of low-bank waterfront, which was inexpensive then. When one of us spotted a log from our front window floating by in the swift current, I hustled out in my 11-foot boat, tied a rope around it, and towed it to our beach. Then I cut the log up for firewood using our 6-foot crosscut saw. Known to old-time loggers as "misery whips," this type of saw had been used for well over a century. Douglas-fir provided the best all-around firewood, so we used little else to heat our house.

As I got older, I noticed that Douglas-fir grew almost everywhere, including on the parched rock outcrops in the rain-shadow zone northeast of the Olympic Mountains as well as in the Olympic Rain Forest, and among subalpine meadows atop mile-high Hurricane Ridge in Olympic National Park. I'll never forget the godsend provided by a big old Douglas-fir growing amid the cliffs of a river gorge in southeastern Olympic National Park. Just out of high school in 1961, two friends and I lost the little-used, partly snow-covered route leading from a high-country ridge down thousands of feet to a safe crossing of the North Fork Skokomish River. We had unwittingly descended in the wrong direction for hours down steep, stony slopes. It was nearing nightfall when we reached the bottom and beheld a frightening sight—a rock-walled gorge containing the roaring river swollen with snowmelt. How could we possibly cross it to get to the trailhead a mile away in dense, untracked forest on the other side, where our parents were waiting?

Finding a safe crossing of this abyss was nearly impossible. We faced the probability that a search party would be called out at dawn and that we would have to backtrack several thousand feet up the steep, brushy slopes with full packs to regain the ridgetop, find the correct route, and then descend to our intended river crossing. Worse yet, there wasn't even a semi-flat spot for an overnight bivouac. Praying for a miracle, I climbed around a corner in the gorge and beheld an unbelievable sight: a 4-foot-thick Douglas-fir growing out of the cliffs had uprooted and lay level straight across the chasm. We had never so appreciated a tree.

In the summer of 1962, I worked at a log-scaling station in the North Cascades. Log trucks brought in huge virgin Douglas-firs from the surrounding forest. Occasionally a truck's 30-ton load consisted of just three massive logs from a single tree, even though these giants had been harvested from steep, rocky mountainsides. Large granite boulders were sometimes jammed into a big log, testifying to the cliffs it had crashed down from. One day a log truck driver let me ride with him up to the logging site carved into granite cliffs. Big Douglas-firs grew wherever there was a patch of soil. Even as an energetic and agile young man, I couldn't imagine how the fallers climbed those treacherous heights with big chain saws and worked there for many hours each day. The guys who measured, limbed, and bucked the logs into the lengths specified by the sawmills didn't have it easy either. Logging in steep terrain was obviously dangerous business.

Later, as a seasonal naturalist in Olympic National Park, I studied some of the gigantic Douglas-firs scattered amid the Hoh River Rain Forest. South of the Hoh, I waded the Queets River to see the famous Queets Fir, which at more than 14 feet in diameter was the largest known Douglas-fir at that time.

The rain forest Douglas-firs were obviously ancient relicts gradually being replaced by younger western hemlock and Sitka spruce trees. I observed the aftermath of a few twentieth-century wildfires that had escaped suppression in the park's mountain forests and saw that many big old Douglas-firs, with their thick, corky bark and lofty crowns, had survived, while associated hemlocks had nearly all died. Also, I noticed that the burned forests had regenerated young trees, especially Douglas-firs, and a rich assortment of fruit-bearing shrubs and herbaceous plants. These post-fire communities teemed with a variety of birds, some of which feed on Douglas-fir seeds, and other wildlife, including black bears, which like to strip and eat the inner bark of young Douglas-firs.

I moved to the inland Northwest in 1963 and then to the Northern Rockies for college and a career in forestry. Forests in these regions were often dominated by other long-lived trees, particularly ponderosa pine, western larch, and western white pine, each with its own unique majesty. Interestingly, inland Douglas-fir nearly always grew in these forests and often regenerated in abundance, filling the understory with saplings and young pole-size trees. Douglas-fir was clearly poised to dominate much of the inland forest.

In 1971, soon after completing a PhD in forest ecology, and keeping mum about that to coworkers in my first job in a sawmill and my second job as a timber-sale forester, I was blessed to be chosen as part of a small research team whose goal was to document examples of the original forest types in the Northern Rockies. We inventoried all trees and flowering plants in 1482 large plots within mature forest stands in Montana and described ecological conditions such as soils, geology, wildlife use, and evidence of past fires. It turned out that Douglas-fir occupied 998 of these stands—a far higher frequency than any other tree or plant. A similar inventory of forests in central Idaho accumulated a sample of 761 stands, 506 of which contained Douglas-fir, again the most frequently recorded plant. Douglas-fir is also widely present and often a dominant tree in forests from central British Columbia to central California and south through the Rockies to the high mountains of southern Arizona. And in all of these regions this species is often one of the biggest trees.

For many years I studied the fire history of old-growth Rocky Mountain forests, consisting of ponderosa pine, Douglas-fir, and western larch. For many centuries, at least, frequent surface fires prevented the highly competitive Douglas-fir from gaining dominance by killing its saplings in far greater numbers than those of fire-resistant ponderosa pine and larch.

I also examined high mountain grasslands and adjacent dry forests dominated by Douglas-fir and lodgepole pine, including the 6500-foot Lamar Valley in Yellowstone National Park. This high, dry grassland environment with its relatively light snowfall serves as critical winter range for the area's elk, deer, and bison, and attracts predators and scavengers such as wolves, ravens, and eagles. Historically, frequent grass fires kept the surrounding forest at bay. Older Douglas-firs tend to be fire-resistant, and some trees at the edge of what used to be an open forest were four or five centuries old and had survived many fires. A few of them measured 4 to 5.5 feet in diameter. But starting early in the twentieth century, two factors allowed Douglas-fir saplings to colonize the Lamar Valley grasslands: fire suppression, and heavy grazing by a burgeoning elk herd that resulted from exterminating the elks' primary native predator—wolves. Nearly a century later, despite the sparse grass fuel, the 1988 Yellowstone fires burned the surrounding and encroaching Douglas-fir forest more severely than most historic fires because of the accumulation of young Douglas-fir thickets and fallen tree limbs and snags.

After sixty years of observing both coastal and inland Douglas-fir and studying their ecology and historical importance, I feel passionate about sharing the story of this truly extraordinary tree. Books and scientific publications have not done full justice to the enormous role the two varieties of Douglas-fir have played in the lives of humans since first contact, nor to the trees' preeminent stature and influence in western forests.

I (Carl) had a distinctly different introduction to Douglas-fir. My experiences started later in life, in a different place, and with the inland rather than the coastal variety. My interactions and perceptions relative to Douglas-fir also differ, but together our perspectives provide a broader and more nuanced story of this enigmatic western tree. Much like two blindfolded men grabbing the opposite ends of an elephant, our initial perceptions reflect our contact with an "elephant" in the plant kingdom that is so widely distributed and variable that it is better described and understood from more than one angle.

My first encounter with Douglas-fir didn't come until I moved west for college, because it isn't native to the Northwoods of Wisconsin where I grew up. I arrived at the University of Montana on a fall afternoon in 1967, hurried over to Main Hall to skim the job listings, and promptly landed part-time surveying work. I started my new job the next morning, and as an inquisitive newcomer, I queried my boss about the unfamiliar trees I saw along our drive to work. I felt somewhat betrayed when he identified several unimposing trees with gray bark and dark green needles as Douglas-firs. I had grown up seeing eye-catching Weyerhaeuser ads of coastal Douglas-fir forests in the 1950s, and frankly these trees didn't measure up. Naively assuming that all Douglas-firs were the large kind, I was unaware of the smaller Rocky Mountain variety. I would later learn that despite their typically modest presence, inland Douglas-fir comprise an ecological time bomb across much of the Mountain West. Over the next fifty years, my work and travels along the backroads of the West would allow me to experience Douglas-fir in two Canadian provinces, eleven western states, Texas, and in virtually all of its native habitats. Seeing the species in its countless manifestations led me to conclude that Douglas-fir is truly the Jekyll and Hyde of the western forest, depending on the time, place, and variety (coastal or inland).

I was drafted by the Army in the summer of 1970 and sent to boot camp at Fort Lewis (now Joint Base Lewis-McChord), about

50 miles south of Seattle. While out on maneuvers one day, I was shocked to see the tops of scattered mature ponderosa pines poking above smaller coastal Douglas-fir. My dismay came from seeing ponderosa pine growing just off the shores of Puget Sound, where it seemingly didn't belong. The much greater precipitation and higher humidity that characterized this coastal site contrasted sharply with the dry conditions where I typically saw ponderosa pine in the Rocky Mountains. Well-drained, rocky soils left behind by receding glaciers likely accounted for the pine's occurrence in this unexpected place. Ironically, coastal Douglas-fir encroachment under the remnant Fort Lewis ponderosa pine presented a tiny, more advanced example of the region-wide phenomenon slowly unfolding in the dry interior West, where inland Douglas-fir had just begun to invade and crowd out the historically dominant ponderosa pine.

I spent the next nearly two years at Fort Ord along the central California coast, often traveling to Yosemite National Park for weekend hikes. It was in Yosemite that I observed Douglas-fir's superior ability to thrive and grow large on what John Muir termed "earthquake talus," slopes of large, nonstationary rocks at the base of cliffs. Although Yosemite marks the southernmost occurrence of coastal Douglas-fir in the Sierra, I saw occasional firs of surprising girth (5 feet in diameter and larger) on the Mist Trail, below Liberty Cap, and along the Panorama Trail.

A 1971 trip to meet a friend in nearby San Francisco included a visit to Muir Woods National Monument and a surprise encounter with Douglas-fir. Muir Woods, located just a few miles north of San Francisco, is a several-hundred-acre enclave of redwoods up to 1100 years old that escaped the first wave of early logging. The monument also boasts a few impressive Douglas-firs, the largest being the massive 280-foot Kent Tree, named after a US Congressman who donated land for the preserve. Despite growing in a redwood sanctuary, the big Douglas-fir was Kent's favorite tree, measuring more than 20 feet taller than the tallest redwood in the park.

After completing military service in 1972, I worked out of a pickup camper as an itinerant research forester sampling regeneration in subalpine forests across the Mountain West. These sites ranged up to nearly 10,000 feet, which established the upper end of an astonishing elevational range for Douglas-firs when compared to the sea-level trees I had seen at Fort Lewis, and provided a real eye-opener for me.

Following graduate school, I took my first full-time job with the US Forest Service Rocky Mountain Research Station in 1980. It was my dream job—travel the interior West and identify broadscale ecological problems on national forestlands from the Canadian line to southern Utah. Field evaluations on dozens of national forests revealed several extensive ecological concerns. One pervasive condition involved thickets, or a layer, of small inland Douglas-fir developing under an overstory of ponderosa pine, ultimately resulting in Douglas-fir dominance and increased threats to stand health and survival. Perhaps because the bottom-up transformation of ponderosa forests to Douglas-fir would take decades to play out, station personnel chose to focus on several other pressing ecological problems at the time.

For this initial assignment, I traveled throughout a wide swath of the interior West, where I also observed Douglas-fir thriving in the dry, cold environments of "island" mountain ranges. Such ranges are typically separated from other mountain ranges and major forested areas by either semi-arid plains or high desert. I found that Douglas-fir often dominated these isolated, high-elevation mountains, where most of the forested zone was too cold for ponderosa pine and too dry for true firs, spruces, or aspen. On lower, less prominent islands, Douglas-fir often dominated at even the highest elevations.

Years later while a forestry professor at the University of Montana, I combed the state's island mountain ranges looking for suitable areas for a graduate student research project. Over previous decades I had hiked much of the Missouri River Breaks and similar topography along several smaller river systems in north-central and eastern

Montana. On rare occasions, I found small individual Douglas-fir trees growing in unexpected places. Their presence on these harsh outlier sites was surprising—far beyond the known easternmost populations of Douglas-fir that grow in central Montana's island mountain ranges. None of the few Douglas-firs I observed were anywhere close to maturity compared to nearby larger ponderosa pines, suggesting that fire kills the majority of these trees while they are still small and more vulnerable to fire than the pines. It also suggests that wind-driven fire rather than lack of water prevents these trees from developing to seed-bearing size. Though the casual observer could easily surmise that Douglas-fir is entirely absent from the eastern Montana landscape, time spent poking around these highly eroded river breaks and coulees may reveal a rare find—a small Douglas-fir growing in a moist microsite, perhaps fed by seepage from an underground spring, but likely surviving only until the next wildfire.

Extensive traveling over the years further sparked my curiosity to visit some of the West's little-known national forests and out-of-the-way national parks and monuments. One such trip included a stop at El Malpais National Monument in western New Mexico, where I was fascinated by the dwarf Douglas-firs clinging to life on nearly barren lava flows. Many of the stunted trees were centuries old but little more than head height. Recalling my earlier visit to Muir Woods, I was struck by the vast differences in growing conditions at El Malpais, yet Douglas-fir were able to grow to old age in both environments. And though both the massive Kent Tree and these elfin Douglas-firs were more than five hundred years old, the giant at Muir Woods was larger in diameter than some of the lava-flow trees were tall and had more than a thousand times the cubic volume. No other tree species on the planet displays such mind-bending contrasts in mature tree size. It is this extraordinary diversity that makes Douglas-fir such an intriguing species, richly deserving of deeper inquiry and broader exposure of its colorful history.

Steve Arno's deep ecological knowledge and experience with both varieties of Douglas-fir, coupled with our history of coauthoring two previous books, provided a strong incentive for me to join him in documenting the life story of this remarkable tree. Readers will find that Douglas-fir is indeed nature's all-purpose tree. It has provided more wood than any other species for building the infrastructure of the American West; its exceptional genetic diversity allows it to have a wider geographic distribution than any other North American conifer; its unique and puzzling combination of characteristics prevented taxonomists from selecting an appropriate scientific name for 150 years; and its longevity and distinct annual rings have allowed scientists to estimate relationships between growth and precipitation extending back more than two thousand years. Finally, before the largest individuals were removed in the early days of logging, historical reports offer substantial anecdotal evidence that coastal Douglas-fir may have been the tallest trees in the world—taller even than redwoods.

CHAPTER 1

Unlocking Douglas-Fir's Secrets

Douglas-fir is an enigma. Its mix of distinctive structural features and physiological attributes produces a tree that is puzzling, exceptional, and in ways a marvel of nature. World class in height, geographic distribution, and wood quality, and unique in architecture and genetic composition, Douglas-fir also acquires nitrogen in novel ways, and at times even irrigates itself. Though this tree has long played an integral role in the lives of humans and animals, many of its secrets are only now being understood through modern science.

Two geographic varieties are recognized, though they exhibit only subtle physical differences. The taller, faster-growing of the two varieties, coastal Douglas-fir (*Pseudotsuga menziesii* variety *menziesii*), occupies the Cascades, Sierra Nevada, and the British Columbia Coast Range, and extends westward to the Pacific shore. Regions to the east are inhabited by the typically shorter inland, or Rocky Mountain, Douglas-fir (*P. menziesii* var. *glauca*), which grows slower and is more cold-tolerant. There are, of course, exceptions. Some habitats within the coastal distribution—such as bedrock sites in the droughty San Juan Islands—support short, limby coastal Douglas-firs, while inland Douglas-firs in moist, wind-sheltered canyons and ravines often grow straight and very tall with little taper.

Because of its much greater size and hence commercial value, the preponderance of scientific inquiry has focused on the coastal rather than inland variety of Douglas-fir. The descriptions, taxonomic difficulties, potential maximum sizes, and water and nitrogen relationships presented here pertain to coastal Douglas-fir unless otherwise noted.

The tree's botanical identity confounded science for more than a century after naturalists first described it—even though its wood was already serving as the world's preferred construction lumber. Douglas-fir was known by more than a dozen common names in the nineteenth century before an official name was finally agreed upon. Selecting a scientific name proved even more elusive. Much drama played out first, and many botanists' dreams of naming the tree were dashed before an acceptable name was found.

Archibald Menzies, a botanist and surgeon who served as naturalist on an early British voyage to the Pacific Northwest, first collected a specimen of Douglas-fir twigs and needles (but no cones) on Vancouver Island in 1791. Menzies did not describe the tree in his journal at the time because he changed jobs when the ship's surgeon fell ill, but Meriwether Lewis described Douglas-fir on his return trip up the Columbia River in 1806. Lewis referred to the specimen he collected as Fir No. 5, which included a written description of the foliage and cones and a drawing of the distinctive cone bract.

David Douglas, the botanist whose name would eventually be adopted for the tree's common name, first arrived in America from Scotland in 1823. The prestige of his association with the Royal Horticultural Society of London opened doors to the finest botanists in the United States, and Douglas made good use of his enhanced access. The timing of his arrival could not have been better. In 1824 the Hudson's Bay Company announced their plans to sponsor a plant collector along the Columbia River, and the young, well-trained Douglas was the natural choice. As a final step in getting ready for his new job in the Pacific Northwest, Douglas arranged to meet Archibald Menzies in London with high hopes of gathering some last-minute advice. When the two men met in the spring of 1824 for a chat over tea, little could they have imagined the role their names would play in the drawn-out process of selecting both a common and a scientific name for Douglas-fir.

Although still early in his career, the energetic and outgoing Douglas had quickly made a name for himself through his association with the Royal Horticultural Society and Hudson's Bay Company, and his acquaintance with many big-name botanists of the time. On his first sponsored trip to the Pacific Northwest from 1824 to 1827, Douglas diligently collected specimens and seeds (including 120 pounds of Douglas-fir seed, equivalent to about three million seeds) from hundreds of plants and trees for later study, classification, and planting back home. His plant collection set a record for the number of species introduced by an individual into England, the leading country in botanical research at the time. Upon his return to London in the fall of 1827, Douglas was welcomed home as a celebrity. The prodigious amount of seeds that he sent or carried back to the Horticultural Society in London overwhelmed the capacity of their gardens for planting, requiring them to engage the help of private nurseries. Douglas-fir seedlings resulting from these efforts were widely distributed to public and private gardens across the United Kingdom. Some of the trees remaining from those early plantings now soar more than 200 feet tall; serendipitously, one such giant grows near Douglas's birthplace in Scone, Scotland.

Given Douglas's celebrity, it is not surprising that in 1833 the English publication *Penny Cyclopaedia* used the name "Douglas Fir" in its description of the species, honoring and acknowledging Douglas as the discoverer "of this gigantic species . . . found in immense forests in North-West America." The *Penny Cyclopaedia* was a companion publication of the *Penny Magazine*, a weekly magazine that sold for a penny to make it widely available to the general public. Both publications were put out by the Society for the Diffusion of Useful Knowledge, whose altruistic intent was to educate the working class in Britain. The newly proposed name gained traction in

Europe but became just one among many other names used in North America in the 1800s.

In 1909 the US Forest Service officially accepted "Douglas fir" as the agency's preferred common name for the tree after a census of western lumbermen found that it was used more than all other names combined. But the search for a universally acceptable common name continued. Coastal loggers favored the name "red fir" because of the tree's reddish heartwood, and many other names were also in use. As late as 1939, Yosemite naturalist James Cole observed, "These magnificent trees from the Northwest are somewhat of a botanical puzzle as indicated by their 28 common names."

Given the hodgepodge of names for this tree that changed over time and place, difficulty in settling on "Douglas-fir" as the official common name is understandable. It wasn't until 1950 that the hyphenated version of the name was formally adopted by the Seventh International Botanical Congress in Stockholm. Even today "Douglas fir"—two words—is more often used in the popular media (including in the title of this book) instead of the correct form, "Douglas-fir," which implies that this distinctive tree is not actually a fir. James Reveal, an expert on the drawn-out process of naming Douglas-fir, found it ironic that the final choice perpetuated a two-part name that is incorrect on both sides of the hyphen. Reveal wryly noted that "This tree is not Douglas's," because someone else first described it scientifically, "and it is not a fir," because the tree's characteristics—such as hanging rather than upright cones and pointed rather than rounded buds—clearly fall outside the description of true firs.

Finding an acceptable scientific (Latin) name for the genus and species of Douglas-fir was even more challenging. Foliage collected by Menzies on Vancouver Island in 1791, plant collections and descriptions made by Lewis in 1806 along the Columbia, and plant materials collected by Douglas on his trips to the Northwest between 1824 and 1830 provided the basis for eighteen scientific names proposed for this species before a suitable name was found.

No other North American conifer even comes close to Douglas-fir in terms of how many names were proposed and rejected before authorities agreed upon a valid name.

The quest began in 1803 when a British botanist named Lambert submitted the first Latin name for Douglas-fir, *Pinus taxifolia*, based on Menzies's sample collected in 1791. The submission was rejected because the name had already been assigned to an entirely different conifer. Seventeen additional scientific names would be submitted over the next 150 years, sixteen of which were deemed invalid because the name had either already been used or did not meet international taxonomic rules. During this period, trees were found in the mountains of Southern California, Japan, and remote reaches of China that shared similarly distinctive cones and other physical characteristics with the widely distributed North American tree. In 1867 a French horticulturist named Carrière proposed putting these geographically dispersed but somewhat similar trees into a new genus, *Pseudotsuga*. By the latter 1800s most taxonomists accepted the new genus name, despite vigorous opposition from a few. One called it "a barbarous combination of the Greek word *pseudo* = false with the Japanese word *tsuga* = hemlock." Another wrote, "One would expect that *Pseudotsuga* would resemble *Tsuga* most of all conifers, but Douglas-fir does resemble this genus least of all." The choice of *Pseudotsuga* ("false hemlock") as the new genus name was indeed puzzling, but the buds, needles, and number of chromosomes of this unusual tree kept it from being placed within existing genera such as pine (*Pinus*), spruce (*Picea*), or fir (*Abies*).

Despite acceptance of the genus name *Pseudotsuga*, attempts to find a suitable species name for this tree remained elusive. Finally, in 1950, Portuguese botanist J. A. F. Franco proposed the currently accepted scientific name for western North America's common Douglas-fir: *Pseudotsuga menziesii* (Mirb.) Franco, honoring Archibald Menzies. (The last name, Franco, identifies the person credited with authorship of the scientific name.) It may seem odd that a taxonomist from Portugal would break the impasse in naming an iconic American tree, but his successful effort is less of a fluke than it might seem. Franco was a distinguished European botanist, credited with authoring the name of 193 plant species over his illustrious fifty-six-year career. The newly proposed name avoided duplication of previously used names and was consistent with the international taxonomic framework for naming coniferous trees. Finally, Douglas-fir had acquired officially recognized common and scientific names. For centuries earlier, Salish peoples along the Northwest coast used the terms *láyelhp* and *čebidac*, among others, as names to identify these trees.

Douglas-fir's genetic diversity, which exceeds that of its associates and nearly all other trees worldwide, accounts for some of its outstanding attributes and sets it apart as a singular species. It has thirteen pairs of chromosomes (called diploids) compared to only twelve pairs (or fewer) in virtually all other conifer species in the Northern Hemisphere, including the other species in the genus *Pseudotsuga*. The physical expression of wide genetic diversity plays out in the tree's uncanny ability to grow on vastly different sites—varying from six-hundred-year-old dwarfs (inland variety) occupying lava flows in the American Southwest to towering 300-foot-tall giants (coastal variety) anchored in the deep, well-watered soils of the Pacific Northwest.

Though the coastal and inland varieties of Douglas-fir merge in southern British Columbia, in the western United States an area of semi-arid grassland and sagebrush east of the Cascades separates the two varieties. The coastal variety occupies the coastal mountains and lowlands south past San Francisco to the vicinity of Monterey, the Cascades and Sierra Nevada south to the moist canyons of Yosemite National Park, and the Lake Tahoe area of extreme western Nevada. Curiously, only the coastal variety inhabits California, while the inland form grows in all the western states except California.

Inland Douglas-fir is abundant in central and southern British Columbia but becomes much less common in the harsh, continental climate of Alberta—where it is confined to lower slopes of the Rocky Mountains and grows only as far north as Jasper National Park. In the United States, inland Douglas-fir is abundant in the mountains of eastern Washington, central and eastern Oregon, Idaho, Montana, and southward throughout the Rocky Mountain chain. It also occurs in the high-desert mountain ranges of Arizona, New Mexico, and extreme eastern Nevada, and in increasingly scattered groves all the way to the tropical mountains of southern Mexico, covering a north–south distance of more than 2500 miles—an exceptionally broad range for any American tree. Variation of the inland variety in isolated mountainous areas of Mexico spurred a proposal in 1949 to add four new species to the genus *Pseudotsuga*. However, genetic work indicates that Douglas-fir migrated southward in Mexico during the Pleistocene Ice Age; isolated populations moved along north–south mountain corridors and occasionally reconnected, but apparently left too little time for any to differentiate into additional species. While the proposal for adding new species was rejected, there is some consensus among taxonomists that the Mexican populations have enough in common, and are sufficiently different from the other two varieties of Douglas-fir, that they deserve recognition as a third variety.

Both coastal and inland varieties of Douglas-fir form tall trees in low and mid-elevation forests within their ranges. For example, coastal Douglas-firs grow from sea level to 3500 feet in northwestern Washington and the inland variety from 7000 to 9000 feet in southern Colorado, New Mexico, and Arizona. Inland Douglas-firs extend upward as shorter trees on south- and west-facing slopes and exposed ridges into the subalpine zone. Sometimes they morph into sheared, shrubby trees in wind-funneling passes along the crest of the Rocky Mountains, and occasionally Douglas-fir takes on the dense, low shrubby form called krummholz above the limit of even stunted, erect trees on high mountain peaks.

Because it adapts to a wide variety of habitats and appears in many forms, no simple description encompasses Douglas-fir. Young trees are the West's most familiar wild Christmas trees. As they continue to grow, young Douglas-firs produce a broad cone-shaped canopy of upward-projecting limbs with abundant branchlets. When they mature, the trees develop an irregular canopy made up of spreading limbs with drooping branchlets that contrast with the more symmetrical branching habit of their true fir (genus *Abies*) associates, such as grand fir (*A. grandis*), white fir (*A. concolor*), red fir (*A. magnifica*), and subalpine fir (*A. lasiocarpa*).

Douglas-fir's needlelike leaves are about an inch long and attached to all sides of the twigs or branchlets, and unlike those of spruce, they are not stiff or prickly to touch. The cones are very distinctive because of the three-pronged, pitchfork-shaped bracts that project from between the scales.

The cones are green at first but turn tan as they mature and grow up to 2.5 to 4 inches long in the coastal variety and somewhat shorter in the inland variety. They are often abundant, and found hanging among the branchlets or lying on the ground. Sometimes squirrels clip off the dense green cones, the size and shape of a small dill pickle, and then gather them up and cache them in a rotten log or underground burrow in order to have a seed supply as winter food. The brownish mature cones dry out on the tree, their scales flex open, and the papery-winged seeds are dispersed by the wind, sometimes several hundred feet. A sticky pitch may be present on both green and mature cones.

When cones aren't available for identification, not even old cones on the ground, the tree's buds are another distinctive feature. They are a rich chestnut-brown color, oval and sharp-pointed, and covered with overlapping papery scales. After the buds burst open in late spring, new light green twigs start to emerge. The bud scales bend backward during this period but remain attached to the previous year's woody twigs. In contrast, buds of true firs and many other conifers are less conspicuous, blunt, light colored, and covered with wax.

The bark of young Douglas-fir trees is smooth, gray, and spotted with pea-size blisters filled with sticky resin. With age the bark becomes rough, and after a century or longer develops into a dark gray-brown corky substance with deep vertical furrows and no resin blisters. Cutting into the bark of a maturing Douglas-fir with a knife exposes wavy bands of contrasting dark brown and light tan. Mature Douglas-firs, such as one-hundred-year-old "second-growth" that sprang up after historical logging, often have a vertical strip of dried pitch on their bark. The bark is also commonly covered with lichens, some a dull dark color, while others may be bright yellow or a beautiful pastel blue-green. Near the base of big old trees, particularly the coastal variety, bark often thickens to at least 6 inches and protects the tree's sap-filled growing tissue from lethal heating by fire, which occurs at about 145° Fahrenheit.

One striking attribute of Douglas-fir is exceptional height. Old-growth coastal Douglas-firs in sheltered valleys commonly reach 250 feet tall and attain diameters of 5 to 8 feet. Occasionally these monarchs tower 300 feet or slightly higher, putting them among a handful of the tallest tree species in the world, surpassed only by the California coastal redwoods (*Sequoia sempervirens*), whose record is a tree named Hyperion, measuring 381 feet. Inland Douglas-fir grows more slowly than its coastal kin due to frigid winters and drought-plagued summers exacerbated by daytime relative humidity of 15 percent or less. Still, in narrow valleys and canyons they can attain heights of 150 to 200 feet.

Centuries-old trees are another noteworthy feature of coastal Douglas-fir forests. Trees greater than five hundred years of age are fairly common, and occasionally trees a thousand years and older have been reported for both Douglas-fir and a number of its associates. The oldest coastal Douglas-fir was believed to be a more than 1000-year-old monarch in Lynn Valley in British Columbia. That trees and forests of this species and its associates have survived for centuries may give the impression that they have been a center-piece of the Pacific Northwest landscape extending back into antiquity. Massive trees, coupled with giant moss-covered logs slowly decaying into the forest floor, seemingly provide visual evidence of sustainable "ancientness." But tree pollen found in sediment layers underlying small ponds across the coastal Northwest paints a different picture. Today's Douglas-fir-dominated old-growth forests first appeared in similar form only about six thousand years ago—a mere blip in the calendar of geologic time. Prior to that time, forest vegetation in the Northwest varied greatly depending on rapidly changing temperatures that occurred 10,000 to 6000 years ago.

Douglas-fir's longevity plays a key role in current efforts to determine climatic patterns (particularly precipitation) over the past centuries and even millennia, providing a baseline for assessing modern-day climate trends. Here it is not the coastal giants but dwarfed, bonsai-shaped inland Douglas-fir trees that have special value.

Growing in the cracks of lava flows at El Malpais National Monument in New Mexico, tiny water-stressed trees survive to amazing ages and their year-to-year growth is highly sensitive to precipitation. Tree rings counted on increment cores show that the oldest known living Douglas-fir at El Malpais dates back 1280 years; another old tree on the flow began life about 960 years ago. These and other centuries-old trees serve as nature's version of solar-powered data recorders, archiving tree-ring widths through good times and bad. Scientists have used the tree-ring patterns (chronologies) to quantify relationships between ring widths and precipitation over the period for which weather records are available.

After establishing such relationships, scientists use tree-ring patterns to estimate annual precipitation in the more distant past. Ancient (subfossil) logs lying on the barren lava flows provide a record of year-to-year tree growth that extends back even further than the living trees. Tree-ring patterns from relict logs that overlap those of old, living trees have allowed scientists to reconstruct a continuous tree-ring chronology—and thereby estimate precipitation—dating back more than 2100 years. Their work shows a period from 1566 to 1608 to be the driest during the last two millennia. Insights provided by the El Malpais tree-ring data suggest that twentieth-century precipitation trends are not outside long-term norms for that area.

Farther south, the Douglas-firs of central Mexico also produce a sensitive, reliable, and long chronology of climatic history. A stand located about 10 miles northwest of 18,500-foot Pico de Orizaba (Citlaltépetl), southeast of Mexico City, is the largest and the least disturbed by woodcutters and by grazing sheep and goats. Some of the trees are five hundred years old, 100 feet tall, and more than 3 feet in diameter. Their growth-ring patterns have been found to correlate well with regional records of spring rainfall and annual yields of maize, the major food crop. A 528-year climatic chronology developed from Douglas-fir tree rings has been used to estimate annual food production from the pre-Hispanic era to modern times.

This tree-ring chronology was also employed in a study of historic typhus epidemics in central Mexico. Typhus, a deadly disease caused by a bacterium transmitted by body lice, occurs where living conditions are crowded and unsanitary. Mexico has written records of typhus epidemics going back to 1655, and the disease historically accompanies famine and war. Documents describe how drought induced large numbers of subsistence farmers to flee to towns for food relief. There, they lived in densely crowded, squalid camps. Historical records were compared with tree-ring reconstructions of growing-season moisture conditions. Below-average tree growth, indicating drought and poor crop yields, occurred during nineteen of the twenty-two typhus epidemics, the most recent of which began in 1915 during the Mexican Revolution.

Detailed analysis of tree-ring chronologies from Douglas-fir and other trees, notably bristlecone pine (*Pinus aristata* and *P. longaeva*), provide a remarkably clear record of climatic variation in many regions of North America. These records are a window to the distant past and are routinely used to accurately date prehistorical events, such as the volcanic explosion that destroyed Mount Mazama and created Crater Lake. They also correlate with ancient records such as the warm climate in Greenland a millennium ago, and centuries later the "Little Ice Age" that devastated European agriculture and resulted in massive famine. Tree-ring records are a living chronology that allows analysis of past and current climatic trends in many areas of the world.

O ne of coastal Douglas-fir's secrets to long life and exceptional height is that it doesn't go it alone. Behind the scenes it gets help from numerous organisms, most of them obscure, and a few even from the animal kingdom. An example that adds further intrigue to Douglas-fir's story is the role salmon play in linking this tree's cycle of life and nutritional needs to the sea.

A nitrogen isotope known as ^{15}N, which uniquely identifies it as coming from the sea, provides a stealth source of this nutrient for the coastal Douglas-fir forest and involves a complex biotic web that resembles a relay team. Salmon from the Pacific Ocean travel upstream along the west coast of North America to spawn in the many rivers and streams that drain the coastal uplands. Bears, coyotes, eagles, osprey, ravens, and other raptors and scavengers are drawn to the easy pickings offered by spawning salmon or carcasses of the spawned-out fish. Gorged on salmon and often dragging or carrying dead fish, these animals move widely throughout the forest, leaving fish scraps and their nitrogen-rich urine and scat to fertilize the soil. Trees, shrubs, and understory plants thrive on the enriched soil and further distribute the nitrogen in the form of fallen needles, leaves, and twigs. This novel animal-plant nitrogen web developed over millennia, with most of the animal contribution moving upstream from the ocean to provide the coastal Douglas-fir forest with a component of its annual nutritional needs in the form of marine-sourced nitrogen. Douglas-fir also obtains some nitrogen from terrestrial sources, made available by soil microorganisms that break down woody material. Another source of this nutrient is rainfall, which sometimes contains nitrogen converted from the atmosphere by lightning. Fires and other disturbances also periodically stimulate nitrogen-fixing plants such as red alder (*Alnus rubra*), Sitka alder (*A. sitchensis*), buckbrush (*Ceanothus*), and lupine (*Lupinus*).

Douglas-fir acquires nitrogen from another kind of biotic partnership, this one with a lichen high up in the tree canopy. Lettuce lichen (*Lobaria oregana*) is a light green fungus resembling garden lettuce that grows in the crowns of large older trees. Lichens are bizarre organisms typically comprised of two fungi and an alga (photosynthetic cyanobacterium) that allow them to process nitrogen gas from the air, which is otherwise unavailable to plants, and convert it into ammonia nitrogen, a form usable by trees. But the trees cannot acquire this nitrogen directly from the lichens. Instead lichens growing in the canopy must be blown or knocked to the ground by wind or snow, where precipitation gradually leaches nitrogen into the soil as the fungi decompose. This pathway sometimes takes a detour when deer or elk eat the fallen lichens, and the associated nitrogen moves into the soil wherever the animals urinate or defecate. The collective contributions are substantial, as lichens can supply an old-growth Douglas-fir forest with a significant portion of its annual nitrogen needs.

Douglas-fir not only survives but flourishes from associations with other organisms in the forest. Some of these biotic partners are belowground, such as two species of false truffle (*Rhizopogon*)— fungi that form mutually beneficial relationships exclusively with Douglas-fir. (Approximately two thousand species of fungi have been identified as potential partners with Douglas-fir.) The fungi attach themselves to Douglas-fir's roots and extract sugars manufactured by the tree to meet their entire energy (food) needs. But the tree also benefits. Fungi that colonize the tree's roots form an expansive mycorrhizal web, or network, that greatly increases the tree's ability to access nutrients and water. Early-twenty-first-century research has uncovered the sophistication of mycorrhizal networks and how they share characteristics with computer information networks. The network connects Douglas-fir trees of different sizes and ages and allows them to exchange food resources, transfer chemicals needed to fend off insects and disease, and share strategies for tolerating drought. Big trees serve as major connection points in these networks, illustrating their importance in forest structure.

Douglas-fir stumps created by logging sometimes provide visual evidence of belowground networking via root-grafting with surrounding live trees. This phenomenon occurs occasionally in the coastal variety of Douglas-fir and can also be found in moister regions of the inland West. Root-grafting is typically indicated when a layer of pitch-like callus tissue forms on the flat top of the stump. The callus tissue acts as a natural sealant that largely protects the dead stump from decay. Because the stump cannot photosynthesize the food (sugars and starches) it needs for callus formation, it has to obtain them from an external source—live, grafted trees. The trees also benefit, as the stump's roots are still alive and physiologically active, extracting nutrients and water from the soil and transporting them to the living trees.

If the grafting relationship lasts more than a year, photosynthate (sugars) from the live trees transported back to the stump may be used to grow a new layer (or ring) of wood around the outside of the stump. The dead stump is somewhat analogous to the dead heartwood of a living tree: both serve as the core around which a new ring of live wood is added each year. A half-dozen such root-grafted Douglas-fir stumps have been documented in the Plumas National Forest in Northern California. The stumps vary in size, age, and time since thinning, but the stump that has so far supported the widest layer of post-thinning growth came from a tree that was 120 years old and 33 inches in diameter at the time of cutting. It had grown a

2.3-inch-wide layer (on average) of live wood around the stump in the eighty-seven years since cutting, illustrating the potential magnitude and longevity of this novel networking relationship. Older root-grafted stumps may even grow a rounded mushroom-like cap that is covered with bark, morphing into a bizarre forest inhabitant seemingly more at place in the domain of elves and goblins than in a Douglas-fir forest.

Another intriguing aspect of Douglas-fir relates to a basic life need: water. Besides living in a region that receives copious precipitation, coastal Douglas-fir forests contribute to their own irrigation. The source of this self-generated watering is the fog that forms over the ocean and then drifts inland, enveloping the forest. Here, the huge canopies of Douglas-fir trees harvest moisture through condensation of water droplets on their needles. Given that a single large coastal Douglas-fir supports millions of needles, what may seem like an insignificant "drip-drip" in a hike through the woods turns out to be a significant contributor to the forest's annual water budget. In the Bull Run Watershed that serves as the water source for Portland, Oregon, fog drip contributes an average 35 inches of moisture, or about one-third of the total annual precipitation.

Scientists continue to delve into the genetic, physiological, and architectural anomalies that make Douglas-fir unique. Increasingly sophisticated measuring instruments and analysis techniques should help shed light on myriad remaining questions and reveal more secrets in the future. The increased knowledge and insights that come from this work, along with the special partnerships Douglas-fir forms with countless other forest organisms, further underscore its status as a world-renowned tree.

CHAPTER 2

Coastal Giants

After his introduction to the Northwest's coastal forests in 1891, pioneering American forester Gifford Pinchot exclaimed, "How utterly dwarfed and insignificant the hardwoods of the East did seem after I had soaked myself in the immeasurable evergreen forests of the West!" Pinchot later became the first chief of the US Forest Service.

Early explorers and settlers encountered a virtually unbroken forest of massive trees extending more than 2000 miles along the Pacific slope from California's Sierra Nevada to southcentral Alaska. From Northern California to southern British Columbia, this temperate maritime forest is epitomized by coastal Douglas-fir mixed with other species of giant conifers, including western redcedar (*Thuja plicata*) and California redwood. Historically this extensive giant forest stretched inland as much as 150 miles to the crest of the Cascade Mountains and was unequalled in extent anywhere else in the world.

As the most abundant tree, coastal Douglas-fir plays a central role in the North Pacific maritime forest. Although the giant sequoias (*Sequoiadendron giganteum*) of the Sierra Nevada and coastal redwoods are goliaths in terms of overall volume, both are confined to narrow habitats only in California, with the minor exception of a few small groves of redwood just across the border in southwestern Oregon. The record-size sequoias and redwoods boast diameters in excess of 20 feet (measured from 4.5 feet above the ground, the

The Queets Fir in Olympic National Park's Queets River valley reigned as the nation's largest Douglas-fir until decay and windstorms in the late twentieth century caused it to gradually deteriorate. Robert Van Pelt describes its decay as very advanced and states that the remaining live branch could collapse anytime, leaving only a dead snag. (Forest History Society, Durham, NC)

standard used in forestry) and trunk volumes of more than 30,000 cubic feet—a volume that could fill four large railroad boxcars. The next biggest trees are western redcedar, Sitka spruce (*Picea sitchensis*), and coastal Douglas-fir, with maximum diameters in excess of 12 feet and trunk volumes of about 10,000 cubic feet, which equates to enough lumber and wood sheathing—plywood and waferboard (OSB)—to build three average-size houses. The Queets Fir in Olympic National Park had the largest diameter (14.46 feet) of any Douglas-fir on record in the United States during the last half of the twentieth century. By 2001 it had lost nearly all of its top and branches but still had one massive living limb. (The tops of exceptionally tall trees often break off in storms. Imagine standing nearby when a treetop the size of a huge live tree comes crashing down from a height of 200 feet!)

North Pacific maritime forests contain several other species of lesser but still remarkable dimensions. Incense cedar (*Calocedrus decurrens*), yellow cedar (*Chamaecyparis nootkatensis*), Port Orford cedar (*Chamaecyparis lawsoniana*), Jeffrey pine (*Pinus jeffreyi*), ponderosa pine (*P. ponderosa*), sugar pine (*P. lambertiana*), noble fir (*Abies procera*), California red fir (*A. magnifica*), and western hemlock (*Tsuga heterophylla*) produce record-size trees 8 feet thick or more. Amid all these giants, however, coastal Douglas-fir stands out because it occupies the most territory, spanning sites ranging from dry and wet lowlands to high mountain slopes.

In terms of height, the tallest living trees are coastal redwoods, with three dozen or more exceeding 360 feet, equivalent to a thirty-story building. The tallest living Douglas-fir, the Doerner Fir in Coos County, Oregon, 3 miles northeast of Sitkum, measures 327 feet, second only to redwoods worldwide. (Other exceptionally tall Douglas-firs might inhabit remote sheltered valleys along the Oregon coast.) The top of the Doerner Fir is reportedly dying or dead. The tree, named for a county commissioner, was originally called the Brummit Fir for its location on the east fork of Brummit Creek. The Bureau of Land Management has created a special trail to it.

In addition to being the tallest living Douglas-fir, the Doerner Fir is notable for apparently being home to the obscure clouded salamander, which is endemic to the Pacific Northwest.

Incidentally, sawmills in the United States today are largely incapable of processing trees anywhere near the size of the old-growth titans, and thus mills don't purchase them. They are also essentially off-limits to logging due to regulations that protect them for a variety of environmental reasons (see chapter 4).

Historical reports provide substantial evidence that several and perhaps numerous Douglas-firs in the 400-foot range once stood taller than any redwoods, dead or alive. Because redwoods have been so thoroughly measured by tree climbers using sophisticated laser surveying technology, authorities believe no taller ones exist. Moreover, a major program to save old-growth redwoods was launched in 1918 by Save the Redwoods League, but the tallest Douglas-firs were logged well before 1918, and the species grows exceedingly tall in numerous areas of the Pacific Northwest.

The most compelling report of a Douglas-fir in the 400-foot range involves the Mineral Tree, so named because it grew near the small community of Mineral, Washington, southwest of Mount Rainier. This giant was carefully measured by prominent foresters in the early 1900s. The great tree's top had broken off in a storm but lay intact on the ground. The height of the standing tree added to the length of the broken top was repeatedly measured by foresters as totaling 393 feet. The tree's standing trunk toppled in 1930, probably from picnickers frequently building fires against it, which eventually hollowed it out. Foresters were able to count the annual growth rings of the fallen giant and determine its age as 1020 years. Measurements of the tree's diameter near its base and its remarkably large diameter at a height of 230 feet made it possible to estimate the trunk's original volume. It totaled about 18,200 cubic feet—far exceeding any known Douglas-fir living today.

An article in a 1910 issue of the *Western Lumberman* reported a huge Douglas-fir east of Seattle that had grown to over 400 feet tall

When this photo was taken, the standing portion of the Mineral Tree was measured to be 230 feet tall. The adjacent broken top was 163 feet long, for a total height of 393 feet when intact, making it the most massive Douglas-fir in the world. (National Archives)

and 17.8 feet in diameter. A 1970 article in the *MacMillan Bloedel News* reported a Douglas-fir felled near Tacoma in early-day logging that measured 412 feet long, plus a stump 5 feet tall, for a total height of 417 feet. Al Carder, who was perhaps the world authority on big trees before he died in 2014, firmly believed that scattered Douglas-firs in the Pacific Northwest were the tallest trees that ever lived prior to heavy logging in the nineteenth and early twentieth centuries. In his book *Forest Giants of the World*, Carder recalls a photo display in the Vancouver, British Columbia, city museum of a Douglas-fir felled in 1902 accompanied by a caption describing the tree's length as 410 feet.

Perhaps the most controversial story of a 400-foot Douglas-fir revolves around a famous, low-quality photograph of a gigantic tree supposedly felled in 1895 in Lynn Valley, now part of North Vancouver. The tree dwarfs the people perched atop its fallen trunk, which they reached via a ladder. Forester John Parminter, who thoroughly researched evidence of this photographed tree, found experts who maintained it was a California redwood, while others were sure it was indeed a Douglas-fir. Some Vancouver-area foresters have evidence that the photo shows a different Douglas-fir giant felled nearby in 1896 that is better documented. Supporting this argument and adding further drama, the man originally credited with felling the 1895 tree claimed he did not do it.

These and other records of 400-foot-tall Douglas-firs from the turn of the twentieth century were probably based on measurements of felled trees lying on the ground and thus presumably subject to little error.

So why aren't there any 400-foot Douglas-firs living today? Forest scientist Robert Van Pelt reasons that the largest and tallest Douglas-firs were prime targets for loggers in the late 1800s or very early 1900s because of their high commercial value and easy accessibility in fertile lowland valleys. Historical photos in dozens of museum collections show people congregated at the base of behemoth Douglas-firs soon to be felled, or a group of people standing on the tree's freshly cut stump. Many other photos show logs from these monstrous trees dwarfing spectators, and document ancient trucks and railcars hauling them.

The question of just how tall coastal Douglas-fir can grow has fascinated big-tree enthusiasts for more than a century. Fortuitously, physiological research sheds some light on this tree's capacity to reach astonishing heights. Transporting water becomes evermore difficult for trees as they grow taller, and scientists generally agree that the species best able to overcome this obstacle has the greatest potential to grow the tallest. To draw a continuous column of water from the soil to the treetop via water-conducting cells, a tree must first overcome gravity and cell-wall resistance (friction). The taller the tree, the greater the pressure it must overcome to transport water and the more likely it is that the water column will break. Douglas-fir possesses specialized cell-wall-thickening tissue arranged in spirals, making its cells stronger than those of most other exceptionally tall tree species. Another important factor is the trade-off between cell-wall thickness and the size of the openings in the cells that allow water to move vertically up the tree. Douglas-fir has a near-ideal balance between the two, giving it an additional advantage in the tall-tree arms race.

In a 2008 study, scientists evaluated cell-to-cell water transport to address the hypothetical question of how tall coastal Douglas-fir can grow, and the results provide evidence supporting early-day measurements exceeding 400 feet. Scientists measured water transport in Douglas-fir trees ranging from sapling-size to nearly 300 feet tall. They then estimated a range of potential maximum heights—where vertical water transport approaches zero—to fall between 358 and 453 feet, the midpoint of which is remarkably similar to historically measured maximum heights of 410 to 417 feet. These scientific estimates coupled with historical measurements exceeding 400 feet provide evidence that Douglas-fir has world-class credentials, whether it be the tallest or second-tallest tree on Earth.

Another interesting feature of the Pacific maritime forest, epitomized by huge Douglas-firs, is its uniqueness worldwide. While other temperate zone forests, like those of eastern North America, consist mainly of deciduous broadleaf trees, the North Pacific maritime forest is dominated by massive evergreen conifers, which sets it apart. Plant physiologist Richard Waring and forest ecologist Jerry Franklin examined research findings, weather records, and other environmental data to identify factors underlying this disparity and discovered that divergent climates play a central role.

The Pacific maritime forest experiences a wet and cool fall, winter, and spring, but summers tend to be warm and dry. In contrast, temperate forests in eastern North America, northern Europe, and eastern Asia have colder winters with periodic incursions of subzero Arctic air. They also have warm, wet, humid summers. That climate favors deciduous broadleaved trees that shed their leaves ahead of the frigid winter. Then, before the warm, moist summer begins, the trees produce their seasonal foliage designed to maximize photosynthesis. In the North Pacific maritime region, deciduous trees are disadvantaged because summers have scant rainfall and relatively dry air. These conditions stress the fragile leaves, which require ample moisture. The leaves of deciduous trees keep cool through transpiration, releasing water vapor through pores—somewhat akin to how people sweat to prevent overheating.

Unlike deciduous trees, Douglas-fir and other conifers have leaves with a small surface area and a wax coating that protects them from overheating and desiccation in summer. Maritime forest conifers cope with dry summers by entering a semi-dormant state, but they retain their foliage year-round and become physiologically active during the cool, moist autumn and spring seasons, and in above-freezing periods in winter, which are typical. Another factor favoring the North Pacific conifers is that heavy, wet snow and sharp frost can occur between November and April. In these conditions broadleaved trees lose their leaves, preventing them from carrying out photosynthesis during the long cool, moist season, but conifer needles, which are small and tough, survive frigid weather, snow, and accumulations of rime ice. The massive trunks and thick sapwood layers of mature conifers enable them to store large volumes of water, which helps them cope with high evaporative demand during warm, dry summers. A single 250-foot-tall Douglas-fir may store more than a thousand gallons of water.

Coastal Douglas-fir and other maritime conifers carry out half or more of their annual growth (carbon assimilation) during the cool fall, winter, and spring seasons. In the wet-winter, dry-summer climate, more of the leaf litter and other organic matter on the forest floor decomposes in the extended cool, wet season. These conditions favor conifers, which are physiologically active and able to capture soil nutrients as they become available. Unlike broadleaf litter, conifer litter is nutrient poor; but Waring and Franklin found that conifers require fewer nutrients than broadleaved trees and use them more efficiently. Also, conifers retain their leaves for several years, dropping only the oldest leaves each autumn, which reduces the amount of nutrients required to produce new leaves each year. About half of the nitrogen needed by a one-hundred-year-old Douglas-fir forest is met by redistribution or withdrawal from older foliage. A broadleaved forest requires substantially more nutrients in a given year.

Long periods between destructive windstorms and wildfires permit conifers, which continue to grow taller in their second and third centuries, to outgrow broadleaved trees. The straight, narrow, conical form of conifer crowns and their fine, slender leaves afford greater resistance to storm damage. Also, big coastal Douglas-firs have thick, corky bark and foliage beginning high above the ground, which provide superior resistance to fire.

Coastal Douglas-firs are abundant and are often the largest trees covering lowlands and mountain slopes from western Oregon to southwestern British Columbia. They occupy sites on deep, productive valley soils as well as rock outcrops harboring only shallow patches of soil. This remarkably adaptive tree also inhabits the Olympic rain-shadow zone, where annual precipitation averages a scant 17 inches, as well as ocean-facing valleys in the Olympic Mountains and on Vancouver Island that are deluged with 150 inches (12.5 feet!) or more. Little wonder, then, that coastal Douglas-fir forests are amazingly diverse.

About 100 miles south of San Francisco, near the southern end of the maritime fog belt, both coastal Douglas-fir and redwoods disappear because of the increasingly hot, dry climate of Southern California. Northward, persistent summer fog allows these trees to absorb moisture through their leaf pores and thus occupy a narrow oceanside strip. In the mountains, the coastal variety of Douglas-fir also ranges southward in California's Cascade Range and the Sierra Nevada. It reaches farther south than its common forest associates, western hemlock, western redcedar, Sitka spruce, and grand fir. Finally, as the Sierra Nevada climate becomes drier, coastal Douglas-fir makes its last stand along tumbling waters in damp, shady canyons of Yosemite National Park, where it still forms a big, imposing tree.

In its northern reaches, coastal Douglas-fir forest extends nearly to the far end of Vancouver Island and in patches to about 53° north latitude along the nearby British Columbia mainland, about as far as the community of Ocean Falls. At this northern extremity it gives way to its principal associates—western hemlock, western redcedar, and Sitka spruce. These shade-tolerant or climax species can grow in the shade of other trees and do not depend on disturbances to perpetuate themselves and ensure their survival. Coastal Douglas-fir is more shade-intolerant, meaning that it needs occasional fires, blow-downs, logging, or other disturbances to create openings for successful regeneration and development.

Thus, coastal Douglas-fir disappears about 100 miles short of the tip of southeastern Alaska, coinciding with the transition to a summer climate no longer characterized by drought. For instance, Aberdeen, on Washington's central coast, receives only about 9 percent of its annual precipitation in the warmest four-month period (June through September), and therefore is prone to summer drought. In contrast, Prince Rupert, British Columbia, roughly 600 miles north along the coast and just past the limit of Douglas-fir, averages 25 percent of its annual rainfall during that same summer period. Moist summers and higher relative humidity in the north contribute to a major ecological change, namely the rarity of forest fires vital for perpetuating coastal Douglas-firs.

Native coastal Douglas-fir forests feature many distinctive types of undergrowth. Some of the driest coastal Douglas-fir habitats feature oceanspray (*Holodiscus discolor*), a tall shrub named for its long clusters of creamy flowers. Slightly more moist forests support a 6-foot-high layer of salal (*Gaultheria shallon*), an evergreen shrub with big laurel-like leaves and clusters of mild but pleasant-tasting berries, and evergreen huckleberry (*Vaccinium ovatum*), which grows to about 8 feet and bears sweet, tiny, dark blue berries. Still moister sites feature the spectacular pink-flowered Pacific rhododendron (*Rhododendron macrophyllum*). This very tall evergreen shrub is often accompanied by nearly impenetrable tangles of vine maple (*Acer circinatum*), whose only saving grace is its beautiful yellow, orange, and red autumn foliage.

On some moist, productive sites the Douglas-fir forest understory is relatively open and dominated by the evergreen swordfern (*Polystichum munitum*), which radiates a luxuriant cluster of shiny, dark green fronds. Great quantities of these swordfern leaves, along with sprigs of salal and evergreen huckleberry, have long been harvested from forestlands leased to professional brush pickers, who carefully bundle them and take them to specialized warehouses that supply this beautiful and long-lasting greenery to florists throughout North America.

In moist forest openings, showy plants abound. In his 1888 essay "The Forests of Oregon and Their Inhabitants," naturalist John Muir rhapsodized about the dazzling burst of color that erupts when one steps from "where the trees grow close and high into a charming wild garden of lilies, orchids, heathworts, roses, etc., with colors so gay and forming such sumptuous masses of bloom, they make the gardens of civilization, however lovingly cared for, seem pathetic and silly."

Pacific yew (*Taxus brevifolia*), a sprawling dwarf conifer with foliage strikingly similar to the giant coastal redwood, forms a forbidding jungle in some understories. Like its close relative English yew (*T. baccata*), which provided Robin Hood and other medieval warriors with wood for their bows, Pacific yew has long been a source of wood for traditional bows. For a few years this tree was the object of frenzied harvesting as a prime source for the cancer drug Taxol. Then chemists discovered how to synthesize the drug, and Pacific yew was again left to its obscure role in the dark forest understory.

Some of these Pacific Douglas-fir understory shrubs, including ocean spray and Pacific yew, along with many of the characteristic herbaceous plants such as swordfern and other ferns, also grow in the wettest parts of the "inland maritime forest" in northern Idaho and northwestern Montana (described in chapter 3). However, in these especially moist inland habitats, Douglas-fir is mostly replaced by maritime conifers, notably western redcedar and western hemlock.

The longevity of old-growth maritime forests favors development of epiphytes—plants that grow in the tree canopies—including many species of moss, some hanging as drapes, along with lichens of many shapes and colors, such as the nitrogen-fixing lettuce lichen. Besides lichens and mosses, old Douglas-firs sometimes support miniature ecosystems in their crowns, including conifer seedlings, huckleberry bushes, and other shrubs that grow on the thick layer of organic material and humus that accumulates on massive limbs high above the ground.

The forest floor may be littered with jackstrawed fallen tree trunks, some as thick as a man is tall and 200 feet long. Such downfalls help create diversity. As logs decay, they serve as nurseries for grubs and ant larvae, which in turn attract animals like woodpeckers and bears. Big pileated woodpeckers with bright red topknots hammer away at rotten logs as well as standing dead trees (snags) in their search for juicy larvae. Old rotten Douglas-fir snags are a godsend for hikers and hunters caught out in a rain- or snowstorm. Even in winter in a sopping wet rain forest, the center of a large Douglas-fir snag contains chunks of relatively dry rotten wood that can be excavated with a small hatchet or hunting knife, and often contains a core of pitch-impregnated wood, which serves as a fire-starter when shaved into strips with a knife.

Stout snags and decaying live trees with broken tops also provide habitat for a host of cavity-nesting birds and small mammals. The reclusive northern spotted owl, averaging about 16 inches long and with a 42-inch wingspan, is one cavity nester occupying old coastal Douglas-fir forests. It was first listed as threatened under the Endangered Species Act by the US Fish and Wildlife Service in 1990, and its status remains unchanged more than three decades later. This owl feeds on small mammals such as flying squirrels and red tree voles—species that also inhabit old-growth trees and snags. Generation after generation of red tree voles can live in a single old Douglas-fir tree, building nests among the branches. The voles eat the needles and obtain water by licking moisture off the foliage.

The marbled murrelet, a small seabird also classified as threatened in Oregon, Washington, and California, depends largely on old-growth forests for nesting. Its habit of nesting in trees was not confirmed until 1973, when a tree climber found an active nest 135 feet up in a large Douglas-fir in California's Santa Cruz Mountains.

Across much of its range, Douglas-fir provides a modest to significant source of winter forage for mule deer. In addition to being the most sought-after big game animal in the western United States, mule deer are also a favorite of wildlife watchers because of their peculiar pogo-stick running style. When startled, they flee in a series of stiff-legged jumps (called stotting), with all four feet hitting the ground at the same time.

In the northern part of the mule deer's range in British Columbia, Douglas-fir makes up the bulk of their winter diet—up to 95 percent on some winter ranges. Browsing is most noticeable on larger trees, where the deer are limited to the limbs they can reach from the ground. This activity leaves an unmistakable horizontal browse line, called high-lining by wildlife biologists, similar to what might be created by a landscaper with pruning shears or a chain saw. Browsing on the lower limbs of larger trees may indicate that more nutritious forage, like native grasses and shrubby willow sprouts, is depleted or covered by snow. The browsing pattern on smaller trees is less evident.

In the late 1980s, scientists conducted a study near 100 Mile House in central British Columbia to evaluate the palatability of foliage from different sizes of trees and from different positions within a given tree. They felled trees from 1 to 20 inches in diameter to allow equal access to all foliage. Foliage from the 16-to-20-inch trees was browsed faster and more thoroughly than that from trees smaller than 12 inches. Surprisingly, foliage on trees smaller than 2 inches went virtually untouched. Scientists believe that deer prefer foliage growing high in the crown of mature trees because of its greater nutritional value. Trees devote fewer chemical defenses to protect against defoliating insects in the upper canopy but more toward nutrition, making the higher foliage that blows down in winter storms particularly preferred forage for deer.

Another animal, the American red squirrel, commonly clips limbs in the upper canopy of mature Douglas-fir trees during winter so that it can consume the nutrient-rich buds later on the ground. This activity also makes the nutritious upper branches, foliage, and buds available as food for mule deer in winter.

Logging of coastal old-growth forests, many of which are dominated by Douglas-fir and most of which are on public lands, has been curtailed since about 1990 due to their biodiversity value and the US Fish and Wildlife Service's classification of the northern spotted owl and marbled murrelet as threatened. According to a

1992 survey, about 7.7 million acres of old-growth forest exist in Oregon and Washington, primarily in national parks and national forests, where it is largely off-limits to logging. Some of that acreage includes high-elevation or other forest types, such as inland Douglas-fir or ponderosa pine. Still, about 2 or 3 million acres of unlogged coastal Douglas-fir forests likely remain west of the Cascade Crest.

Efforts to preserve coastal Douglas-fir forests tend to ignore the important ecological influence of primeval fire. For more than ten thousand years, soon after the last ice age, fire had a major effect on most of these diverse forest communities. The coastal Douglas-fir relies on fire to suppress its more shade-tolerant competition. During the twentieth century, fire's role in shaping forests was largely eliminated through suppression. To perpetuate the long-lived coastal Douglas-fir forest, conservationists must acknowledge the need to plan for fire or to substitute comparable disturbances, and land managers will need to carry out such plans (see chapter 7).

CHAPTER 3

Inland Douglas-Fir: Fixture of the Mountain West

While the coastal variety of Douglas-fir is the superstar of the Pacific Northwest forest and the pillar of the lumber industry, its morphologically similar cousin, interior Douglas-fir, is an underappreciated Cinderella. The ubiquitous inland Douglas-fir is valued for lumber, firewood, and wild Christmas trees. Considered a utilitarian tree, it lacks the charisma linked to old-growth coastal trees as well as its associates in the inland forest: ponderosa pine with its striking cinnamon-colored trunk, western larch (*Larix occidentalis*) with its summer lime- and then autumn gold-colored foliage, western white pine (*Pinus monticola*) with its long sausage-shaped cones and neatly checkered trunk, western redcedar with its low lacy boughs, or Rocky Mountain white fir (*Abies concolor*) and Colorado blue spruce (*Picea pungens*) with their splendid bluish foliage.

Compared to these and other iconic trees of the Mountain West, inland Douglas-fir seems a plain Jane. Even worse, it is often deemed a nuisance or even a villain largely because fire suppression has allowed it to form dangerously crowded stands and displace important trees, shrubs, and grasslands. Meanwhile, many of inland Douglas-fir's more remarkable characteristics go unnoticed.

For example, this tree has an unparalleled ability to succeed in an immense variety of habitats throughout the West. It adopts different forms depending on conditions: it may develop a huge columnar trunk where it soars out from a moist mountain ravine, or support a dense canopy of gigantic limbs that nearly sweep the ground when it grows atop a high windswept ridge.

Douglas-fir's coastal and inland varieties are distinct genetically but exhibit only minor differences in foliage, cones, and physical appearance other than size. West Coast trees grow larger than their inland counterparts primarily due to a more favorable climate. Needles of inland Douglas-fir often have a slightly bluish-green cast, while coastal trees are yellowish green to dark green. Also, cones of inland Douglas-fir tend to be shorter (1.5 to 3 inches long) than those of coastal trees, and the three-pronged bracts that extend beyond the cone scales spread or flex outward on cones of inland trees, whereas cones of coastal trees have bracts pressed forward along the scales. However, the two varieties overlap in north-central Washington.

Both varieties are generalists that inhabit a broad array of habitats, but interior Douglas-fir surpasses its coastal cousin and all other forest plants in this regard. While coastal Douglas-fir flourishes in a temperate maritime climate, inland Douglas-fir succeeds in incredibly harsh sites where winter temperatures can plummet to −70° Fahrenheit (as recorded at Rogers Pass, Montana) and places where summer temperatures climb to 110° Fahrenheit. It inhabits moist, productive forest soils, raw lava flows, parched desert-edge sites, and cold subalpine mountains, as well as most places that lie between. Inland Douglas-fir is second only to its frequent companion ponderosa pine in drought tolerance, but it is better adapted to survive the extreme cold that restricts ponderosa's distribution. It has the greatest latitudinal range of any North American conifer. It extends from near the boreal forest in north-central British Columbia southward through the Rockies and scattered desert peaks of the Southwest and Mexico, eventually showing up as an isolated population in tropical mountains of southern Mexico.

As mentioned in chapter 1, Douglas-fir has an extra pair of chromosomes not found in any other species in the Pine family, including true firs (*Abies*), pines (*Pinus*), spruces (*Picea*), and hemlocks (*Tsuga*). Research confirms that inland Douglas-fir's many genetic forms (genotypes) are key to its ability to thrive across a gamut of environments. Growth characteristics such as dates of bud burst in the spring and rate of growth seem to be linked to local environmental conditions. For example, radial growth of centuries-old Douglas-fir trees in Montana correlates strongly with precipitation received during the current growing season and from July through October of the previous year. Old Douglas-firs continue to photosynthesize into this late summer–early fall period, but they transition from using the photosynthate for growth to storing it for use the following spring. Interestingly, one 9-inch-diameter tree in this study was found to be more than eight hundred years old.

Inland Douglas-fir is so widespread and successful that it has acquired a Jekyll and Hyde reputation. On the one hand, it is acclaimed for its contribution to human and wildlife habitats and for valuable lumber and other products. On the other, it is faulted for converting mountain grasslands to tree thickets and crowding out aspen groves and riparian broadleaf trees and shrubs critical for wildlife. It also produces dense understories in historically open ponderosa pine forests, increasing the pine's vulnerability to insects, disease, and wildfires. In fairness, these troublemaking traits are caused mostly by the policy established with the founding of the US Forest Service in 1905, which disrupted the ecological role of fire and failed to substitute controlled burning and other treatments for primeval fires (see chapter 6).

In moist and riparian habitats, inland Douglas-fir grows rapidly, but without fire, logging, or other disturbance, it is eventually crowded out by more shade-tolerant species like grand fir, western redcedar, western hemlock, Engelmann spruce (*Picea engelmannii*), and subalpine fir. In northern Idaho and the adjacent parts of Washington and Montana, it is a member of what foresters call the

Shown here in 1936, the Ruby River valley in southwestern Montana hosts large 300-year-old Douglas-firs that have survived multiple fires. The shorter aspens surrounding them date back to the last fire. (Archives and Special Collections, Mansfield Library, University of Montana)

North Idaho Mix—the richest and most productive forest of the inland West. In addition to inland Douglas-fir and the previously mentioned shade-tolerant species, the North Idaho Mix contains western white pine, lodgepole pine (*Pinus contorta*), ponderosa pine, western larch, mountain hemlock (*Tsuga mertensiana*), quaking aspen (*Populus tremuloides*), black cottonwood (*Populus trichocarpa*), paper birch (*Betula papyrifera*), water birch (*B. occidentalis*), and alders. In Idaho Mix country, Douglas-fir often grows fast and dies young, succumbing to root rot fungi in less than a hundred years.

However, along streams in most of the inland West, Douglas-fir can survive for 250 to 300 years and form a splendid columnar trunk towering 125 to 150 feet high that rivals the accompanying Engelmann spruce. The largest known inland Douglas-fir, 6 feet in diameter and 178 feet tall, grows near the Thompson Lakes in northwestern Montana. Record-size inland Douglas-firs in Idaho, eastern Washington, British Columbia, and southeastern Arizona are approximately 5 feet in diameter and 150 feet tall or more. A 5.3-foot-thick, 163-foot-tall Douglas-fir grew north of Durango, Colorado, but was killed in a 2018 wildfire. Forest scientist Ronald Lanner reports finding centuries-old stumps of similarly huge Douglas-firs in northern Utah's Wasatch Mountains.

On dry forest sites, inland Douglas-fir is classed as intermediate in shade tolerance but more tolerant than its associates. Therefore, unlike on moist habitats, Douglas-fir becomes dominant when a dry forest remains undisturbed by fire or logging over long periods. On the most arid sites, scrubby Douglas-firs and limber pines (*Pinus flexilis*) 15 to 20 feet tall form a dwarf woodland directly beneath the steep eastern edge, or escarpment, of the Northern Rockies in Montana. This "elfin forest," interspersed with aspen groves and flowery meadows, forms a narrow transition zone between the Great Plains grassland and the Rocky Mountain forest, and provides prime forage and cover for a variety of wildlife, including grizzly bears. By comparing historical photographs to modern images, it is apparent that this elfin forest has expanded, most likely as a result of fire suppression. In this area west of Great Falls and Cut Bank, Montana, but unlike 100 miles farther north at the foot of the Rockies in Alberta, Douglas-fir is also abundant up to moderately high elevations in the mountains.

Perhaps the best way to appreciate the adaptability of inland Douglas-fir is to hopscotch through the kaleidoscope of its environments along a 2500-mile transect from boreal Canada to southern Mexico. In the north its limits lie east of Hazelton, British Columbia, where it meets the southern edge of the boreal forest that extends across northern North America and is the counterpart of far northern forests in Europe and Asia.

Douglas-fir reaches past the northern limits of its common associates, ponderosa pine and western larch. At the northern edge of its range, it is accompanied by quaking aspen, paper birch, subalpine fir, and lodgepole pine—trees that occupy both the temperate and boreal zones—but it also mixes with the distinctly boreal white spruce (*Picea glauca*) and black spruce (*P. mariana*) that spread hundreds of miles farther northward to the edge of the treeless tundra. The Takla Lake Ecological Reserve in British Columbia, at a latitude of 55°20' north, features the northernmost Douglas-fir stand that covers about 150 acres on hilly slopes above the lake. The trees average about a hundred years old and 100 feet tall. Their surprisingly vigorous growth suggests that inland Douglas-firs can spread even farther north, especially if global warming continues.

Climate modeling projects that by 2085, Douglas-fir will more than double (124 percent) its current acreage in British Columbia, while disappearing from only 10 percent of its currently occupied habitat. These changes are projected to occur rapidly, with Douglas-fir moving northward into new habitat at an estimated 60 miles per decade and reaching the province's northern border by 2085. Most of Douglas-fir's increase is projected to occur in the interior plateau country, where it will likely colonize existing boreal forests.

Southward in the interior of British Columbia, the climate becomes less exposed to Arctic cold waves, and trees characteristic of the middle latitudes prevail. In wet, snowy regions like the Selkirk Mountains, traversed by the Trans-Canada Highway at awe-inspiring Rogers Pass, shade-tolerant species, such as western redcedar, western hemlock, Engelmann spruce, subalpine fir, and mountain hemlock, dominate the forest. Here, Douglas-fir is a pioneer that colonizes areas opened up by wildfires, avalanches, and logging. But in the extensive dry regions of central and southern British Columbia, Douglas-fir seems omnipresent.

Douglas-fir dominates forests that surround native grasslands of the Cariboo-Chilcotin country near Williams Lake, 200 miles southeast of its northern limit. From there, Douglas-fir mixed with grasslands spreads southward 250 miles to the Okanagan Valley just north of the US border, which features Canada's mildest, sunniest climate. This broad inland region, called the dry interior Douglas-fir zone, extends eastward through the interior cedar-hemlock zone to the 1000-mile-long Rocky Mountain Trench. The trench is a remarkable U-shaped valley squeezed between towering mountain ranges to the east and west. The southern part of the trench is drained by the Kootenay and Columbia Rivers and supports dry Douglas-fir forests and grasslands. The region is home to the oldest western ranches in Canada and a ranching culture that dates to the early 1870s, when it was opened for homesteading.

Major areas of British Columbia's dry interior Douglas-fir zone have been invaded by thickets of young Douglas-firs. Relicts of the original forests, including large old stumps, indicate that up until the turn of the twentieth century much of this region consisted of more open stands dominated by mature trees, some of which had scars from frequent low-intensity fires. Historical stands were scattered among bunchgrass prairies. Today, in cooperation with local ranchers, the British Columbia Ministry of Forests conducts thinning and prescribed burning projects to help restore the open forests and grasslands.

On the eastern slope of Canada's towering Rocky Mountain Divide in Alberta, Douglas-firs are confined to limited favorable sites due to the harsh climate. Winter brings sudden invasions of Arctic air (–30° Fahrenheit or colder), often when there is little snow to insulate tree foliage or roots. Then warm, dry Chinook winds abruptly roar in from the west, raising temperatures into the 50s. The sun heats foliage of evergreen trees even further, but roots and tree trunks remain frozen or chilled and unable to replace moisture lost through transpiration. Inland Douglas-fir is more resistant to these winter drought conditions than ponderosa pine and many other western trees, but less resistant than the boreal forest species. As a result, the northernmost Douglas-firs in Alberta reach only 53° north latitude, in the Athabasca Valley near the town of Jasper in the Canadian national park bearing the same name. Open Douglas-fir and grassland communities hug the south-facing slopes in this spectacular mountain-locked valley. Chinook winds sweep the slopes, melting snow, exposing forage, and providing snow-free shelter beneath spreading Douglas-fir canopies, thus creating winter range for elk, moose, deer, and bighorn sheep. Park managers also employ prescribed fire to substitute for the low-intensity fires that maintained the open forest and grasslands in centuries past.

South of the Canadian border in the inland United States, Douglas-fir's distribution could be parodied by the country-and-western song "I've Been Everywhere." In the vast region lying east of the Cascade Mountains and west of the Great Plains as far south as northern New Mexico, inland Douglas-fir is so widely distributed in forests and woodlands that its *absence* anywhere seems noteworthy. For instance, it is locally absent from some of the driest ponderosa pine forests on basalt geology west of Spokane and on droughty pumice in central Oregon. Also, it doesn't occupy the highest-elevation wet forests, the domain of Engelmann spruce and subalpine fir. Still, a few wind-pruned, shrubby Douglas-firs eke out an existence on southern exposures at the uppermost limit of trees.

Craters of the Moon National Monument and Preserve in south-central Idaho provides an example of Douglas-fir's extreme hardiness in a drought-plagued site. The otherworldly flows of black lava at Craters of the Moon are dotted with bizarrely shaped limber pines and scrubby juniper (*Juniperus*). However, a keen observer will note that wind-sheltered sites support small groves of straight Douglas-firs. Similarly, individual Douglas-fir trees can also be found in the vast and inhospitable Missouri River Breaks of central and eastern Montana, where the flat to undulating shortgrass prairie is disrupted by innumerable gullies and coulees, a few harboring adequate subsurface moisture for Douglas-fir to establish. Douglas-fir is at its drought limit virtually everywhere else in this remote region.

Where they haven't been logged, stands containing stocky, thick-canopied inland Douglas-firs form the lower timberline on mountains rising high above the 6000-foot valley floors in eastern Idaho, southwestern Montana, western Wyoming, and northwestern

Colorado. Douglas-fir groves mingle with sagebrush-grassland on slopes above popular attractions in the high valleys, including Steamboat Springs, Colorado; Jackson Hole, Wyoming; Sun Valley, Idaho; and the restored ghost towns of Bannack and Virginia City in Montana. In some of the driest mountain ranges, patches of Douglas-fir are virtually the only trees, and it is possible to hike on grass-and-sagebrush-covered slopes all the way up to the alpine tundra without passing through any trees at all.

At the US border with Mexico, Douglas-fir extends 1000 miles southeast from its sizeable communities in the mountains of Arizona and New Mexico. Its distribution in Mexico is puzzling. Only the inland form is present, and it occurs in small, isolated populations widely scattered among the two principal mountain ranges, the Sierra Madre Occidental and the Sierra Madre Oriental. These amazing Douglas-firs were discovered in 1994 by scientists from Hungary and China at about 9000 feet in elevation in a dense, junglelike forest, mixed with three different Mexican pines and several subtropical oaks and other trees. Some of these trees attain diameters up to 2.5 feet, and they can grow 100 feet tall, suggesting that they do well here. Remarkably, the southernmost known Douglas-firs inhabit a tropical mountain forest at 16° north latitude above the city of Miahuatlan in the Sierra Madre del Sur in southern Mexico, much farther south than any other North American tree.

Larger communities of Douglas-fir are situated about 120 miles farther north in sheltered canyons and on moist north-facing slopes at about 10,000 feet in elevation in the Sierra Madre Oriental of northwest Orizaba. All of the southern Mexico populations are believed to be relicts of a more extensive distribution of the species in the highlands of Mexico during the last ice age. The government of Mexico lists Douglas-fir as "subject to special protection." Since Mexico's Douglas-firs are geographically isolated from the much larger US populations by a vast region of desert, it is not surprising that they differ from their US counterparts morphologically and likely genetically.

Unfortunately, all populations of Douglas-fir in central and southern Mexico are threatened by human encroachment and climatic warming. Most of these stands are small, fragmented, and exhibit scant reproduction, perhaps related to inbreeding, domestic grazing of livestock, and a marginally adequate climate. As a result, although inland Douglas-fir is remarkably ubiquitous and successful in the western United States, its status near its southern range limits in Mexico is tenuous.

Mountain grasslands with scattered Douglas-fir trees, called savannas, and more dense, well-stocked pure stands of Douglas-fir with grassy undergrowth were once widespread at higher elevations throughout much of the Intermountain West. Growing conditions in these areas were near ideal—neither too dry nor too wet. Both Douglas-fir savannas and well-stocked stands grew on high ridges and sunny, south- and west-facing slopes, occupying entire regions that are evidently above the cold limits of ponderosa pine. Though few of these Douglas-fir communities remain, remnants of both types can be found near the road that passes through the northern part of Yellowstone National Park at Mammoth and Tower Junction and bordering the Lamar Valley.

The largely snow-free and wind-sheltered area within and beneath the crowns of these open-grown trees provides a refuge for many animals. Blue grouse eat the tree buds during winter and roost in their dense canopies, sheltered from storms, raptors, and other threats. Cylindrical sawdust-like pellets expelled by grouse litter the ground below. Mountain chickadees, nuthatches, and Canada jays are just a few of the birds that make use of the stout Douglas-firs in winter. Red squirrels nest in the trees and store prodigious quantities of cones in middens beneath them. When the cone crop is abundant, Clark's nutcrackers eat Douglas-fir seeds and cache some in the soil for later use. If they are left unretrieved, these cached seeds sometimes grow into new trees.

Unfortunately, many of these formerly open stands now contain thickets of young trees. Remnants of the old stands undoubtedly still occur in north-central Washington, western Montana, western Wyoming, and central Idaho. In some scattered areas the old Douglas-firs weren't completely logged off or killed by wildfires or bark beetles. These places still retain a few of the stout ancient trees, 3 to 5 feet in diameter and up to four centuries old.

In the few remaining savannas, old Douglas-firs have broad, low canopies of huge branches. They cast shade over a circle up to 50 feet across, and their expansive root systems seem to prevent thickets of young trees from squeezing in close; instead, native pinegrass (*Calamagrostis rubescens*), elk sedge (*Carex geyeri*), and bunchgrasses cover most of the ground beneath the trees.

In times past, periodic grass fires were instrumental in keeping thickets of young trees from taking over. Although a century of fire suppression contributed to the loss of the big old Douglas-firs, most of them were cut down in the early mining era or removed by loggers throughout the twentieth century. Many of the remaining stands were logged in the 1960s and 1970s when demand for national forest timber was high. Then Congress passed the National Forest Management Act of 1976, which required that logged federal lands be regenerated within five years. The native grass and sedge turf in the logged areas of drier forests made prompt tree regeneration virtually impossible. To remedy this situation, foresters stripped away the sod layer with bulldozers. This practice amplified the environmental campaign against the clearcutting of mountainsides and bulldozing of terraces that had begun several years earlier.

Wildlife biologists, foresters, and ecologists have recognized the environmental threats created by Douglas-fir encroachment in former communities of sagebrush and grassland. Thickets of young trees shade out forage grasses important for wildlife and livestock. They also displace sagebrush, reducing habitat for sage grouse, a big, showy bird whose declining populations make it a candidate for protection under the Endangered Species Act. Douglas-fir invasion also increases the risk of severe wildfires that spread to adjacent forests and to homes, cabins, and critical wildlife habitat. Combined, the 2002 Rodeo-Chediski wildfire and the 2011 Wallow wildfire destroyed 20 percent of the threatened Mexican spotted owl nests that exist in the world, primarily in Douglas-fir–mixed conifer forests in Arizona. Because of these devastating events and growing threats, national forest managers and Nature Conservancy land stewards have cut the young trees and used prescribed fire to counteract tree encroachment in some areas. However, the scope of this problem is daunting (see chapter 7).

An immense variety of undergrowth vegetation is associated with inland Douglas-fir throughout the West. The robust shrub called ninebark (*Physocarpus malvaceus*), with its constantly shedding bark, makes it hard to traverse many Douglas-fir forests in the inland Northwest. On dry sites, ninebark's small maple-like leaves turn bright orange or red during late summer. Productive but frost-prone valley bottoms, as well as the nearly flat terrain called benchlands, are often carpeted with luxuriant dwarf huckleberry (*Vaccinium caespitosum*) and kinnikinnick (also called bearberry, *Arctostaphylos uva-ursi*). These ground-hugging woody plants have tough vine-like stems that take root as they spread. Amateur horticulturists are likely to rue the day when they transplanted kinnikinnick as an evergreen ground cover, because in cultivation it can spread far and wide and be hard to control. In native forests its resin-rich foliage was often trimmed back by surface fires, and it resprouted from underground stems called rhizomes.

Both kinnikinnick and dwarf huckleberry produce little fruits that feed grouse and other small animals. Kinnikinnick fruits look like tiny red apples, about the size of a garbanzo bean (chickpea), and are especially valuable for wildlife because they remain edible on the plants for months. Kinnikinnick may be the most widespread plant in inland Douglas-fir forests, and it ranges clear across North America and parts of Eurasia as well. It forms a "turf" in some of the moist Douglas-fir forests, as well as those on droughty fragmented limestone where even dryland grasses are scarce.

Many of the common western trees and undergrowth plants are absent from limestone rock substrates because the coarse soils they produce are excessively well drained and alkaline, in contrast with most conifer forest soils, which are acidic. However, inland Douglas-fir tolerates almost all soil types, and thus by default dominates high-elevation limestone sites that under more common soil conditions would be occupied by lodgepole pine, subalpine fir, and spruce. The road wandering east toward Yogo Peak along the broad 8000-foot-high crest of central Montana's Little Belt Mountains, for example, leads through a lodgepole pine and subalpine fir forest with an understory dominated by the low-growing huckleberry shrub called grouse whortleberry (*Vaccinium scoparium*). The road traverses an acidic rock substrate, and then suddenly the vegetation changes to a Douglas-fir–grassland community with a rich assortment of flowering herbs. This abrupt boundary marks the road's entry onto limestone soils.

Nearby steep south slopes on fragmented limestone feature Douglas-fir mixed with limber pine and whitebark pine (*Pinus albicaulis*). Patches of kinnikinnick and the limestone-associated horizontal juniper (*Juniperus horizontalis*) form the primary ground cover, along with a few hardy cushion plants normally confined to the alpine tundra. These Douglas-fir communities also feature some plants that grow only on limestone, including both a columbine and a clematis with spectacular deep blue flowers.

Inland Douglas-fir is common in limestone formations at Utah's Bryce Canyon National Park despite the dry climate. The trees are most abundant in the southern, higher elevations of the park, at 8000 to 9000 feet, but can also be found in shady sections of Bryce Canyon's main amphitheater. The most famous Douglas-firs stand squarely on the narrow trail threading through the bottom of the deep slot canyon called Wall Street, where they soar skyward, presumably reaching for the sun.

Majestic aspen groves are a trademark of the productive high country in central Utah, western Colorado, northern New Mexico, and the White Mountains of Arizona, and they rely on fire to regenerate. Groves of big aspens are often overtopped by scattered, much larger Douglas-firs that survived historical surface fires, which would also have stimulated "suckering" (a form of resprouting) from the aspens' underground roots. Today, largely as a result of fire suppression, aspens are declining and not effectively regenerating, while more shade-tolerant Douglas-fir, spruce, and subalpine fir that grew up as understory trees are gradually crowding them out (see chapter 6).

CHAPTER 4

The Tree That Built an Empire

When David Douglas traveled to the Pacific Northwest in the 1820s, he described coastal Douglas-fir as "one of the most striking and truly graceful objects in nature," and added what turned out to be a classic understatement: "The wood may be found very useful for a variety of domestic purposes."

The West Coast timber industry originated in the 1850s in the Puget Sound region of what was then Washington Territory, where the area of big-tree forest roughly equalled the entire state of Wisconsin or Florida, and vast expanses of massive Douglas-firs lined the Sound's labyrinth of navigable waterways, making it easy to log, mill, and ship from many lumber ports. By the early 1900s, Douglas-fir had come to symbolize a world-renowned timber industry centered in the Pacific Northwest. Logging, milling, and exporting lumber from virgin forests dominated by giant Douglas-fir would comprise a major component of the region's economy into the 1980s. As nature writer William Dietrich describes it, Douglas-fir "was the sacred center of forest capitalism, the money tree, the sawmill dream." The industry continually transformed itself over this period, but by 1990 it was forced to refocus and emphasize management of much younger "second-growth" trees in previously logged forests.

The impetus for Northwest sawmilling was the California gold rush. By December 1849, the port settlement of San Francisco teemed with fortune seekers lured by gold in the Sierra Nevada foothills nearly 100 miles to the east. Lumber was urgently needed to build accommodations and infrastructure, in far greater quantities than nearby mills could produce. San Francisco's surroundings, which were largely covered with grassland, short limby oaks, and other broadleaved species of similar stature, couldn't yield sufficient volumes of suitable timber. The huge redwoods as well as Douglas-firs that grew along the rugged coast north of San Francisco Bay weren't accessible via natural harbors. The mountain forests located in the rugged Sierra Nevada and Coast Ranges also remained inaccessible to roads that could support heavy freight wagons or other means of transporting large volumes of logs or lumber over steep, rocky terrain.

Sky-high demand and prices for lumber enticed entrepreneurs to search for sawmill sites on bays accessible by ship and surrounded by big timber. The closest one to fit the bill was Humboldt Bay, 250 miles north of San Francisco. By 1853, several mills had begun sawing logs from the giant redwoods and Douglas-firs surrounding the bay. However, as with nearly all estuaries opening directly to the tempestuous North Pacific Ocean, Humboldt Bay's entrance was largely blocked off by a hazardous shoal and sandbar. Despite the valiant efforts of local pilots and tugs, 12 of the 143 sailing ships hauling lumber out of the bay in 1853 wrecked while attempting to cross the bar. Additionally, furious winds, fog, and pounding surf often kept these ships bottled up in the harbor for days to weeks before they even chanced an exit. The bay's treacherous entrance also required use of small vessels with a shallow draft that could haul only small loads of lumber.

The account of the *Southerner*, a steamship ferrying mail and passengers to ports along the Pacific Northwest Coast, illustrates the problem of entering the shoal-guarded harbors, even for a small steam-powered craft far more maneuverable than the large windjammers preferred for hauling loads of lumber at the time. In December 1854, the *Southerner* was able to enter Humboldt Bay to service Eureka and soon afterward to dock at Crescent City, near the border with the Oregon Territory. A howling gale and huge swells kept it from getting into Port Orford or the Umpqua River's mouth to the north, or past the treacherous bar at the opening to the Columbia River. Swells pounded the ship, which soon took on water. With all pumps working, the captain headed 150 miles north toward the Strait of Juan de Fuca, the broad entrance to Puget Sound in the Washington Territory. Passengers bailed with buckets and tossed cargo overboard. At daylight on December 26, they sighted land 26 miles south of Cape Flattery at the entrance to the Strait. The ship kept taking on water. The captain dropped anchor in shallow water off a stretch of sandy beach along the jagged coast. High seas broke across the deck and dragged the ship broadside into the beach. The crew cut away the mast and smokestack to keep the wreck upright. Then, fortunately, the tide went out, allowing all hands and passengers to escape to the shore. A few hours later the tide rose again and smashed the ship to smithereens.

Before the lumber trade became established in the Northwest, Captain Charles Wilkes of the US Navy seemingly foresaw the solution that would later provide San Francisco with an ample lumber supply. During an 1841 visit to Puget Sound, Wilkes described its potential as a port: "Not a shoal exists within the Straits of Juan de Fuca, Admiralty Inlet, Puget Sound or Hood Canal that can in any way interrupt their navigation by a seventy-four-gun ship." The broad and deep Strait and Admiralty Inlet form an easy entrance to a maze of storm-sheltered, navigable waterways and natural harbors. Moreover, most of Puget Sound's 1300-mile shoreline at the time was surrounded by lowlands covered with giant coastal Douglas-fir, often accompanied by smaller amounts of valuable western redcedar.

With San Francisco's increasing demand for lumber in the 1850s, many enterprising individuals were lured by the promise of Puget Sound. According to an 1895 historical chronology of the seafaring business in the Pacific Northwest, "Reports of the remarkable possibilities for marine business . . . on that vast inland sea, Puget Sound and its tributaries, had spread among the mariners on the more crowded waters of the Eastern coast, and they came with the rush."

Frederic and William Talbot and A. J. Pope were among the first and most successful developers of what would become a lumber industry that depended on huge volumes of easily accessible old-growth Douglas-fir in Puget Sound. Although they were new to the San Francisco lumber trade, they came from long-established saw-milling families in Maine. In June 1853, Captain William Talbot sailed into Puget Sound to locate a site suitable for a sawmill. Even from a distance, the crew was struck by the towering Douglas-fir forest, the symmetry of the massive trees, and their cinnamon-brown trunks. Dropping anchor and rowing ashore in Discovery Bay, the party measured fallen trees 250 to 280 feet long and up to 12 feet thick at the base.

After exploring several promising coves in the northern part of Puget Sound, Captain Talbot settled on Gamble Bay near the tip of the Kitsap Peninsula. With milling equipment hastily shipped from New England around the perilous tip of South America, Pope and Talbot completed construction of their new Puget Mill in September 1853, joining a handful of other small mills sawing boards from nearby Douglas-firs. Within a few years more than two dozen sawmills appeared in Puget Sound, many built by investors in San Francisco, which is where the boards were shipped almost as soon as they were cut.

The Kitsap Peninsula and adjacent Bainbridge Island, in the center of Puget Sound, emerged as the hub of the new lumber empire. Despite this area's isolation from land transportation, excellent water access to big timber and numerous natural harbors made it ideal for lumbering. By the mid-1800s, five of the nation's largest sawmills and several smaller ones were running in Kitsap County (which includes Bainbridge Island), making it one of the richest counties per capita in the United States.

The first timber for milling in Puget Sound came from clearing the actual mill sites and their immediate surroundings. More came from lands cleared by pioneers drawn to the area by the Donation Land Claim Act of 1850, which offered 320 acres per person, or 640 for a married couple, if the land was "improved upon" and occupied for five years. When settlers cleared the land for farming, the logs were skidded to the water, collected into log booms, and towed to mills by contracted tugboats.

Small boats plying the Sound's relatively calm waters were essentially the only form of transportation in the area. Building even a rudimentary network of wagon roads through the thick, wet forests would take decades, whereas year-round water transit in the Sound was immediately available. Soon after settlements appeared in the 1850s, a hodgepodge of small steam-powered boats began transporting passengers and freight throughout Puget Sound and north to the San Juan Islands and southwestern British Columbia. Some of the boats were built from the readily available Douglas-fir lumber. The steamboats were so numerous that people said they resembled a "swarm of mosquitoes" and referred to them as the "Mosquito Fleet."

In response to the frenzied 1898 Klondike Gold Rush, a commercial water-transport network reached north from Seattle and Tacoma via the Inside Passage to service the hinterland of the Yukon and southeastern Alaska. In the prior year, between January and March, 18 vessels left Seattle for Alaskan ports, but in the same period of 1898, 173 ships cleared Seattle headed for Alaska. The ships that carried much of the early Alaskan traffic were built from Puget Sound's Douglas-fir. Today's major international shipping terminals at Seattle and Tacoma originated from the 1850s attraction of Puget Sound for milling and exporting Douglas-fir lumber.

A commercial empire centered around the splendid and easily accessible Douglas-fir forest in Puget Sound provided lumber to North America's West Coast and soon thereafter to countries across the Pacific and eventually worldwide. By the 1860s, the Strait of Juan de Fuca and associated northern inlets also supported a fledgling lumber export industry on southern Vancouver Island and the adjacent southwestern British Columbia mainland. For the next one hundred years, no other industry came close to matching logging in terms of economic importance to the Northwest coastal region, stretching from Northern California to southern British Columbia—an industry featuring old-growth Douglas-fir.

I t's difficult to imagine the discomfort, endurance, and hazards associated with the daunting task of logging massive Douglas-firs, some of which towered thirty stories high and were about as wide as a compact car is long. What's more, nineteenth-century loggers typically worked six twelve-hour days per week, often in wet brush or in rain or slushy snow that dumped on them as they felled trees. Their job conditions were a recipe for hypothermia.

Taking down the giant trees involved many tasks, beginning with making way for skid trails by clearing brush that often grew in tangles taller than a man. In the early years, logging was concentrated within about a mile of tidewater, since that was the practical range for skidding with slow-moving teams of oxen. The men who cleared the skid trails were known as "swampers."

Next, two "fallers" climbed onto spring-boards several feet above the ground, placed in notches cut into each side of a giant tree's trunk using axes. (A few remaining old-growth stumps in Pacific Northwest forests still display these notches.) Then they felled the tree using a "misery whip," an astoundingly long two-man cross-cut saw, fabricated from shorter manufactured saw blades welded together end to end to create one giant blade at least 12 feet long. Historian Stewart Holbrook explained that the main reason for

A logging crew poses on and around a large Douglas-fir in King County, Washington, in a photo taken circa 1900. Men with axes stand on spring-boards on each side, while between them crew members pose in an undercut made with double-bitted axes, which severed about 30 percent of the tree trunk. The large saw propped against the tree was used to create the backcut that felled the tree. (C1949.1224, Washington State Historical Society, Tacoma)

falling the Douglas-fir from a tall stump was to avoid the copious flow of sticky pitch that would pour from a cut near the base. Fallers often remained standing on the spring-boards when the tree crashed to the ground. If the tree's trajectory went askew, it might carom off another tree and crush a faller. Or any of the huge limbs might break off and crash atop the faller, who in those days didn't have even a hard hat. All of this work required tremendous skill as well as good luck. (Small wonder scores, if not hundreds, of loggers were killed on the job every year. Even now, despite great advances in safety, logging remains one of the most dangerous occupations in the world.)

"Buckers" would then chop the limbs, often 10 inches or more thick, off the fallen trees and cut the trunks into desired log lengths using the misery whip. Limbs on the bottom side of the tree posed a special problem. They were pinned beneath the multiton log, some having broken and jammed deep in the ground. Access to these limbs required rolling the log, probably using oxen. Imagine the exhausting process of crawling through tangles of massive limbs, some weighing hundreds of pounds, and somehow clearing them away with an ax. Then picture having to cut logs from the 6-to-10-foot-thick trunk with a long cross-cut saw raised high, all while balancing on branches. To complicate matters, it was necessary to continually pound heavy steel wedges farther into the top of the cut and slather the saw with kerosene to keep it from "binding," or being pinched by the heavy and pitchy logs. After the buckers finished their work, teams of oxen, yoked in twos up to twelve pairs, dragged logs down greased skid trails to the water's edge.

The whole process could be compared to the enormous task the Lilliputians conducted in tying down the giant in Jonathan Swift's *Gulliver's Travels*. But this is the sort of work loggers performed for long hours day after day in the old-growth Douglas-fir forests.

Logging camps consisted of a primitive, cramped bunkhouse and mess hall that could be moved from one cutting operation, known as a "logging show," to the next. Men slept in crowded rows of bunks sometimes stacked three high (terrifying for anyone prone to claustrophobia!). These were clammy, foul-smelling quarters due to wet, sweaty clothing hung over the ends of the beds and sopping leather boots crowded near the central woodstove. (Imagine the nightly snoring from a large number of exhausted men packed into this confined space.) Some logging crews slept in dorms mounted on floating barges towed from one site to another and secured to a makeshift dock. Logging camps were rough-and-tumble, male-dominated environments offering little entertainment. Perhaps the only pleasures were the hearty meals provided at the cookhouse tables—where the workers gulped down food and coffee without conversation, as talking was not allowed during meals at most camps. On their one free day each week, drinking, gambling, fighting, and carousing with prostitutes in nearby towns were common pastimes. However, some loggers relished a quiet day off, perhaps remaining at camp in a comfortable place to simply read or study, recognizing that in a short time logging would take a tremendous toll on their bodies. Being alone and far from their families, those men who didn't advance to better jobs would likely face a bleak future.

A few mill owners, including A. J. Pope and William Talbot, sought to improve order and mill efficiency by establishing company-controlled towns. In 1861 they began purchasing tracts of Puget Sound timberland, which by 1864 totaled more than 32,000 acres. The company provided a hotel for single men and visitors, cottages for married workers, a cook hall, company store, school, church, baseball field, and sometimes a saloon. A writer who visited these mill towns in the 1860s and 1870s described them as "feudal" because of the complete authority and autonomy of the mill owners.

The 1880 Census states that "The leading and most profitable industry of Puget Sound is lumbering. [Douglas] Fir forests completely cover the face of the land to the water's edge.... There are 15 or 20 saw-mills at different points ... and lumber camps have been established near them, often within a stone's-throw of the water's edge. The ship-yards have all been established in the saw-mill towns.... The nearness to the mills enables a [ship] builder to order the timber as fast as he needs and to save the cost of transportation."

The market for Puget Sound lumber developed rapidly in the 1850s. Just as water transport was key to Puget Sound sawmilling, it was also crucial to marketing the lumber. By the late 1850s, the still small Puget Mill was loading more than sixty vessels per year, including shipments to such exotic destinations as the Hawaiian Islands, Sydney, Melbourne, Hong Kong, and even Tahiti. During the next three decades, hundreds of ships transported lumber from Puget Sound and many other Northwestern ports to various destinations along and across the Pacific Ocean. By the early 1880s a triangle trade had developed, with Northwest lumber shipped to Australia, Australian coal to Hawaii, and Hawaiian sugar to San Francisco. The return trip to Northwest lumber ports was made with a heavy ballast such as bricks manufactured near San Francisco. Some of the sailing vessels were privately owned and others belonged to logging companies. By 1880 a fleet of five to ten sailing ships was constantly loading lumber at Port Gamble, and Pope and Talbot owned most of them.

Like logging, this seafaring work was hazardous once ships left the friendly confines of protected inlets and entered the North Pacific, where the stormy, craggy coast between San Francisco and Vancouver Island was dubbed the Graveyard of the Pacific.

In late autumn of 1860, two lumber ships wrecked in storms off Cape Flattery, a rocky peninsula jutting north at the mouth of the Strait of Juan de Fuca. One was the Peruvian brig *Florencia*. Upon entering the Pacific, the ship was pounded for a week by powerful winds. "She floundered like a dead whale, all hands clinging desperately to keep from being thrown into the surging tempest." In desperation the crew cut loose the deck load of lumber and the masts, but still greater waves swept the deck, sending the captain, a passenger, and the deck cargo to a watery grave. The now de-masted ship sprang back on an even keel and drifted north onto deadly rocks off Vancouver Island.

About the time news of the *Florencia* tragedy reached Puget Sound, another ship arrived and reported sighting pieces of wreckage from the American ship *John Marshall* off Cape Flattery. She was long overdue to pick up a load of lumber for San Francisco and

Schooners like the Wawona *were built of Douglas-firs milled from Pacific North-west forests and then used to transport Douglas-fir lumber around the world.* (Puget Sound Maritime Historical Society, Williamson Collection, 10781)

was last sighted off the cape battling a howling gale. Nothing more than fragments of wreckage were found, and apparently the entire crew perished.

At first, in the early 1850s, lumber was hauled with East Coast vessels, largely old square-rigged sailing ships with bulky topsails. These ships were hard to load with long, heavy boards, and large crews were required to manage the sails. Soon West Coast ship-yards sprang up and designed specialized vessels known as lumber schooners. By the early 1880s, the design of West Coast lumber ves-sels had become well established and differed radically from ships built in New England. Schooners without topsails eliminated the need for climbing aloft, since all the sails could be tended from the deck. Because lumber is a bulk cargo that does not require shelter and is difficult to stow belowdecks, lumber schooners were designed to haul a large part of their load on the deck. They were typically built of the same Douglas-fir as the lumber they carried—usually 2 inches thick, although the hulls were often made of extra-heavy 3-inch-thick planks. In 1920, near the end of the windjammer era, the largest lumber-hauling sailing ship was built and christened *Oregon Pine*, an early common name for Douglas-fir. It was a schooner with six masts that could transport almost 2.25 million board feet of lumber (a board foot is equivalent to a board 12 inches square and 1 inch thick)—enough to build about 180 three-bedroom houses, and far exceeding the lumber capacity of New England ships. It was 267 feet long and 50 feet wide, with a draft of 25 feet.

Because lumber schooners did not need to be built with a deep hold, average-size schooners had a shallow draft and were able to avoid sandbars. Development of lumber schooners along with construction of rock breakwaters and dredging of shoals boosted lumber shipments from the Northwest harbors that open directly onto the Pacific Ocean, such as Grays Harbor in Washington, the mouth of the Columbia, and Coos Bay in Oregon.

At first the oceanfront ports in Oregon shipped huge volumes of giant Sitka spruce, also known as tideland spruce, the major tree growing along the nearby lowlands. Long before the availability of cardboard or plastic, lightweight spruce boards were in high demand for shipping crates and boxes for orchard fruit and canned salmon. They were also valued for siding and other purposes where strength and durability were not required, and by World War I they were sought after for airplane framing. However, once logging railways reached the old-growth Douglas-fir forests in the coastal mountains above the ocean ports, Douglas-fir lumber exports soon exceeded those of spruce.

The 1880 Census reported eleven shipyards in the Washington Territory, all of them on Puget Sound and its bays and inlets. The ships were built from old-growth Douglas-fir whose great length allowed shipwrights to build large ships with long hulls from single boards rather than butting the ends of two or three boards together as was necessary in New England shipyards. This single-board construction gave the hull greater elasticity and reduced the risk of springing a leak. Durability and decay resistance were also attributed to Douglas-fir ships, while for mast and spar timber, coastal Douglas-fir was acclaimed to have no superior in attributes and no equal in size.

Some of the biggest ships were built at Seabeck on Hood Canal (a natural, glacier-gouged channel connected to Puget Sound), including the *Olympus*, which in 1880 was the largest single-decked ship in the world. The deck was 223 feet long, her beam (or maximum width) was 43.5 feet, and the keel was a massive 20-by-48-inch timber. She was built for hauling lumber and carried loads up to 1.45 million board feet. In her first eleven months, the *Olympus* earned $40,000 (roughly equivalent to $1 million today) in freighting, which paid back half the ship's cost.

Wooden steam schooners started taking over the West Coast lumber trade in 1884. Underpowered and stacked high with lumber, these ships were tasked with the difficult and dangerous mission of navigating amidst the storm-lashed Northwest Coast, especially at night or in the frequent fog or pouring rain. Of the fleet of more than two hundred schooners, about 75 percent left their weathered skeletons on perilous stretches of the Pacific Coast. They traveled dangerously near the shore to skirt rock islands and reefs and darted in and out of tiny "dog hole" ports to retrieve loads of lumber.

The *Protection* was one of the original steam schooners, built in 1888. Although relatively small at 281 tons (and probably about 130 feet long), for a decade she packed enough lumber to build a small city. On December 29, 1899, she left her Seattle dock loaded with lumber for San Francisco. Heading down the coast, she hit a New Year's Eve storm somewhere off the mouth of the Columbia River, and at last report was swept over by mountainous waves. She disappeared with all aboard, nothing more was heard, and not so much as a scrap of wreckage was ever found.

Steam-powered vessels continued to gradually replace sailing ships, and steel hulls gradually replaced Douglas-fir planks. Still, at the turn of the twentieth century, many steamships were being constructed with Douglas-fir. Shipwrights learned to use Douglas-fir that had been cut in fall or winter, because trees cut earlier in the year contained sap that made their lumber vulnerable to rapid decay. Shipbuilding experts said that sap-free Douglas-fir lumber, if salted, would endure as long as oak.

At the same time, several factors converged to vastly increase Northwest lumber production and exports, which continued to be dominated by coastal Douglas-fir. Records show that from 1892 through 1910, Douglas-fir lumber shipments from Pope and Talbot's Port Gamble Mill to San Francisco and other West Coast ports exceeded lumber from all other species by a ratio of more than thirty to one. Arrival of transcontinental railroads to the Northwest in the 1880s and 1890s was followed in the early 1900s by successful negotiation of favorable freight rates for shipping lumber to the Midwest. Thus in 1905, for the first time, rail-shipped lumber exceeded ocean-borne cargo. Between 1906 and 1907, mills in Grays Harbor on Washington's Pacific Coast filled big orders for transport by railroad, while also loading 600 steam- and sail-powered timber-hauling ships.

When Portland and Astoria, Oregon, began shipping large quantities of Douglas-fir and other lumber to foreign and Midwest markets as a result of improved ports and expanded railroad access, timber barons used fraudulent land claims and poaching to obtain timber on unprotected federal lands in Oregon's Coast and Cascade mountain ranges. This timber theft, often aided by corrupt officials, alarmed President Theodore Roosevelt's administration and helped spur the 1905 transfer of federal forestland to a newly created US Forest Service, headed by Gifford Pinchot.

By this time timber from the Great Lakes and eastern states was largely depleted, and Northwest timber was in demand in the Midwest and the eastern United States. Builders found Northwestern Douglas-fir superior for framing and other structural purposes due to its greater strength, board quality, and availability in larger and longer dimensions, including beams up to 24 inches thick and 100 feet long.

A lthough by the early 1900s steel hulls had replaced wooden ships as the standard for ocean shipping, World War I ushered in two fleets of wooden ships, many of which were produced from Douglas-fir at Northwestern shipyards. In 1916, Assistant Secretary of the Navy Franklin D. Roosevelt ordered the design of a small antisubmarine vessel that could be built quickly in small commercial shipyards, reasoning that if the United States entered the war, major shipyards would be needed for building larger warships. As a result, 441 wooden subchasers were put into service and equipped with armaments, including a depth-charge thrower, and many had hydrophones for detecting underwater noises. They were 110 feet long, with a 14-foot, 9-inch beam, and a top speed of 18 knots (about 20 miles) per hour.

When the United States entered the war in April 1917, the US Shipping Board concluded that the country didn't have enough ships to carry supplies, food, and ammunition to support US troops. Although wood was considered obsolete for large ships, the urgent need for cargo ships and the ability to build wooden ships much faster than steel hulls, especially using coastal Douglas-fir, put many Northwest shipyards to work.

The Emergency Fleet Corporation contracted for 703 Ferris standard wooden steamships 281 feet in total length and with a maximum beam of 45 feet. Because US involvement in the war lasted only about one and a half years, just 323 of the ships—less than half—were actually constructed. After the armistice was signed in November 1918, most of the Ferris ships were either sold for scrap or left to rot in Mallows Bay, now part of a national marine sanctuary along the Maryland coast. A number of the obsolete ships were used to form breakwaters along both the Atlantic and Pacific, including a half-dozen at the mouth of the Snohomish River near Everett, Washington. The sinking of the Ferris ships symbolically ended the tradition of using wood for oceangoing freighters—a tradition that had started in the 1400s when European mariners first ventured around the southern tip of Africa to trade for coveted spices and silk in the Far East.

Although wood had become obsolete for freighters, in 1940 John Steinbeck chartered a 77-foot fishing boat with a hull built of old-growth Douglas-fir and set off for the Sea of Cortez in an attempt to escape the fame and controversy generated by his 1939 book *The Grapes of Wrath*. His principal companion was a quirky ecologist named Ed Ricketts. The book Steinbeck produced as a result of their freewheeling adventure, *The Log from the Sea of Cortez*, is funny but also a serious account of overfishing and other environmental abuses, and was Steinbeck's favorite. The boat sank four times during its lifetime, the last time sitting submerged in a bed of muck for nearly six months. Finally in 2013 it was hauled to the surface, by which point it reportedly looked like a ghost ship. The derelict was towed west from its saltwater graveyard near the entrance of Puget Sound to the storied home of Douglas-fir shipbuilding, Port Townsend, Washington, to be restored. An article in the September 2019 issue of *Smithsonian* magazine reported that although rebuilding the rest of the ship required mostly new materials and a few million dollars, the old-growth Douglas-fir hull was still sound.

S tarting in the late nineteenth century, timber harvesting technology advanced rapidly and made it feasible to log more of the rugged Northwestern landscape, not just areas near navigable waters. Prior to that time, much of Oregon's vast old-growth Douglas-fir forest on the east slope of the coastal mountains and high up in the Cascade Range had been inaccessible to loggers, thus the state ranked behind Washington and California in lumber production. However, Oregon's ranking as a timber producer would improve over the coming decades with the introduction of new harvest systems and technology.

Starting in the 1880s, one such system burst on the scene, and it would dominate logging until the 1920s. This new system, called a steam donkey, was mounted on skids and employed large cable winches powered by a steam engine. The steam donkey provided a quantum leap forward in the efficiency and reach of timber harvest, opening up new country previously too difficult to log. A lumberman in Grays Harbor, Washington, gushed that steam donkeys "require no stable and no feed," and with "no teams to winter, no ground too wet, no hill too steep, it is easy to see they are a revolution in logging." The donkey engine could be towed from place to place, anchored, and used to skid big logs efficiently over long distances. Temporary, portable logging railroads were established and moved as needed to collect logs and transport them to navigable waterways, roads, or established railroad lines.

"High lead" cable logging systems introduced in the 1920s used aerial pulleys mounted on a live Douglas-fir, which was converted to a "spar tree"—a sort of derrick—by removing its limbs and top. The 150-foot-tall spar tree was braced with guy cables with another cable running through a pulley atop the spar to drag or "yard" logs up steep slopes, across ravines, and over rough terrain. The elevated pulley lifted the front ends of logs off the ground to minimize friction and prevent them from jamming against stumps or boulders.

The spar tree rigger's job required tremendous skill and daring, even when compared to other jobs in the hazard-prone world of logging. He climbed the Douglas-fir's huge trunk by digging into its thick bark with steel spurs strapped to his boots. For support he had to lean back against a rope that he thrust around the trunk. He also had to flip the heavy manila rope upward repeatedly as he climbed and circled around the trunk to hack off dozens of big limbs with

A caravan of logging trucks transports sections of mammoth Douglas-fir, possibly all from a single tree, through the town of North Bend, Washington, east of Seattle, in the 1940s. (Forest History Society, Durham, NC)

his ax. When he finally de-limbed the tree to a height where it was about 3 feet in diameter, he felled the multiton top by applying the technique that ground-based fallers use to guide the direction of a tree's fall. If the top fell the wrong way, it could easily crush him as he clung to the trunk. It's no wonder the spar tree rigger was considered the consummate symbol of skill and stamina.

During the 1920s, Caterpillar crawler tractors became popular for skidding logs substantial distances on slopes up to 60 percent. Bulldozer blades mounted on the tractors carved out rough logging roads that could be accessed by increasingly bigger and better logging trucks. The five-ton White Motor Company truck with solid rubber tires that premiered in 1912 was one of the first.

By the 1930s most of the Puget Sound basin's virgin timber had been milled, and better railroad access, road building, and logging systems vaulted Oregon to the top spot as a timber-producing state.

As logging technology continued to advance over the next several decades, the timber industry was able to expand deeper into western Oregon, western Washington, and southwestern British Columbia, where old-growth coastal Douglas-fir was still abundant in the more remote and mountainous terrain. At first most of this big timber came from lands granted to railroads and from other industrial and private timberlands, but after 1950 increasing proportions came from national forests and other public lands. Improved equipment and more efficient road-building and harvesting techniques facilitated access to the remaining virgin forest. The post–World War II era ushered in chain saws, mechanical tree harvesters, portable spar towers, and other specialized yarding techniques including cranes, helicopters, and blimp-size balloons. The upswing in demand for construction lumber—for which Douglas-fir was ideally suited—surged as new home construction boomed after the war, and as houses and other buildings became ever larger.

Traditionalists like Gifford Pinchot considered virtual liquidation of old-growth forests outside of national parks and a few natural areas good forestry. These utilitarian foresters wanted to replace slow-growing old-growth forests with young, fast-growing, managed stands. By the 1970s and 1980s, graphic evidence of disappearing virgin forest confronted even the casual observer who recoiled at views of huge, stunningly obtrusive clearcuts on mountainsides visible from major highways, recreation areas, and airplanes.

At the same time, previously unknown and unacknowledged functions and values of old-growth forests were being discovered and publicized by ecologists and wildlife biologists, and new environmental laws, including the Endangered Species Act, were being implemented. By 1990, changing public sentiment and court decisions to protect old-growth habitat for sensitive and endangered wildlife species largely eliminated logging of old-growth forests on public lands. The most high-profile example of this change in forest management focused on protection of the northern spotted owl, which the US Fish and Wildlife Service judged as dependent on undisturbed old-growth habitat for food, shelter, and successful breeding. The ruling that triggered the end of more than a century of old-growth logging fueled a series of battles that played out in the media, in courtrooms, and in heated arguments among the public at large. It also profoundly affected the volume of timber harvested from Northwest national forests and the jobs associated with its removal.

By 2001 annual timber harvest on national forestland nation-wide had plummeted to about 20 percent of its 1960 to 1990 aver-age, largely due to protection of Northwestern old growth. Logging old-growth reached its peak in 1983. Since 1990, national forest harvesting has remained at low levels. Rapidly declining timber harvest accompanied by increasing mechanization has led to huge losses in timber-related jobs. Employment in the timber industry, which in 1990 totaled 65,000 in Oregon alone, shrunk to less than half that level by 2010. In the 1960s and 1970s, 10 to 12 percent of Oregon's gross domestic production was contributed by the wood products industry, but by 2010 this had fallen to less than 2 percent. Part of the dramatic decline in wood products employment, par-ticularly at mills, can also be attributed to a surging export market beginning in the late 1980s. Whole logs and cants (squared logs) from second-growth Douglas-fir and other species were shipped to Japan, where lumber prices were far higher than in the United States. At times the insufficient supply of logs available to domes-tic mills has been due to the ability of Asian buyers to outbid them.

Rather than liquidating the remaining old growth, an emerging consensus has sought to perpetuate or re-create a semblance of his-torical ecosystems using several strategies: specially designed har-vesting techniques that leave big trees and snags and create open-ings for regeneration to simulate the effects of fire; management of younger forests to facilitate development of old-growth conditions; and the use of fire where possible (see chapter 7). By the year 2000, the timber-driven economy of the coastal Northwest had given way to a new, diversified economy where younger stands of Douglas-fir and other conifers were a major component, and the wood products industry was constantly innovating to adapt to highly volatile national and international markets.

CHAPTER 5

Douglas–Fir Use Through the Ages

North American Indian tribes have lived in relationship with Douglas-fir since the earliest of times, based on both folklore and archaeological evidence. The Tewa people of New Mexico, for example, claim that humankind first came to Earth by climbing up a tall Douglas-fir tree from under a lake. Another legend recounts that Southwest Indians planted a Douglas-fir tree to ascend to Earth through an opening in the roof of the underworld, but it didn't grow tall enough, so they planted a sturdy reed to climb instead.

Indians in the Rocky Mountains and Southwest prized interior Douglas-fir for its many uses, and tribes of the Pacific Northwest considered coastal Douglas-fir subordinate only to western red-cedar as the "tree of life." Both varieties of Douglas-fir historically fulfilled myriad roles for native peoples and were the overwhelming choice for one critical daily need: fuel for their fires. This preference was not simply due to the trees' ubiquitous presence in coastal forests or their accessibility in most interior forests but likely resulted from long-term experience using Douglas-fir and other species in many different heating and cooking scenarios. Independent tests by the US Forest Service Forest Products Laboratory have quantified what native peoples observed over millennia: the heat values of Douglas-fir bark exceed those of associated tree species, whether bark or dry wood. Bark was especially favored for smaller cooking fires in enclosed areas because it provided ample heat for cooking, produced little smoke, and didn't spark.

Firewood in driftwood form was a close and self-replacing source of fuel for Northwest Coast tribes, whether for shellfish processing or more general cooking or heating purposes. Like the bark, Douglas-fir driftwood was also a superior fuel. Douglas-fir charcoal has been found by archaeologists at nearly all historical shellfish-processing sites despite a ready supply of other kinds of wood. A comparison of twenty different species of driftwood recovered along the northern Pacific Coast found that even in this form Douglas-fir has a higher heat value than any other species.

Douglas-fir also supplied materials for countless other specialized tools or applications in the form of small trees, branches, twigs, needles, roots, knots, pitch, cones, and even ashes. Native peoples living in the northern interior, for example, crafted Douglas-fir saplings into hunting bows and sturdy snowshoe frames. On the coast, people used parts and pieces of Douglas-fir to construct a remarkable range of implements for catching fish. Sapling-size trees were used to make rakes for gathering small fish such as herring and smelt, or shaped into handles and hoops for various kinds of fishing nets. Spears and harpoons were also made from smaller Douglas-firs to harvest sea urchins and seals or to place bait in desirable positions to catch codfish. Short pieces of heartwood infused with pitch were used as torches during night fishing. Some tribes boiled the bark to produce a brownish dye that made fishing nets less visible. Coast Salish peoples steamed Douglas-fir knots so they could be bent and crafted into large, sturdy hooks. Archaeologists found that some of the massive hooks carbon-date back nearly two thousand years. Although the ancient hooks were unearthed while excavating along the freshwater Little Qualicum River in British Columbia, historians believe they were used to fish for cod on nearby saltwater fishing grounds.

Douglas-fir was also used for building fishing weirs to capture salmon as they moved up coastal rivers during spawning season.

Posts made from pole-size trees held the weirs in place, and saplings were cut into pieces and placed vertically in a dense array that resembled a picket fence. The stakes slowed the fish as they moved upstream, while scattered openings in the weir diverted them into traps or nets. Well-preserved remnants from a Douglas-fir weir were discovered under layers of sand at Nehalem Bay along the northern Oregon coast. A mat woven from Douglas-fir roots recovered at the same site radiocarbon-dated back about 380 years. Saplings were also crafted into long handles needed for the large dip nets used to catch fish during the annual salmon runs, particularly where natural obstacles slowed their movement upstream.

Coastal indigenous peoples used Douglas-fir bark as a preservative for storing spiny dogfish, an unsavory option during winter when other fleshy foods were scarce. They gutted the dogfish (a kind of small shark), stuffed the carcasses with pulverized Douglas-fir bark, and then buried them under powdery, rotten fir wood. When needed, they recovered the preserved dogfish and washed and then slowly barbecued them over Douglas-fir coals in a final step to help offset the nausea-inducing oil in the shark.

Native peoples in Northern California, and likely elsewhere, used Douglas-fir boughs as seasoning for barbecuing venison and elk, and Indians living in the Great Basin built fires from the branches when barbecuing bear meat. Salish people of the interior Northwest also used rotten Douglas-fir wood as the preferred fuel for building fires to smoke animal hides. The boughs were also widely used to cover the floor of sweathouses and for temporary beds while camping.

Salish in the Northwest scrubbed their skin with Douglas-fir twigs and needles to cover their scent before hunting. They also peeled the twigs and tied them in bundles for use as "whippers" to efficiently knock berries off buffaloberry (commonly called soapberry, *Shepherdia canadensis*) bushes. Berries were whisked with a whipper into a foamy substance used as shampoo or soap, which had both cleaning and astringent qualities and left the skin feeling fresh and clean. Some California Indians used fir twigs as a coarse warp (or vertical element) in baskets, while others used the small roots in basket-making.

Douglas-fir pitch was a favored firestarter, especially in wet weather. It was also used to patch leaks in canoes and to seal containers used for carrying water. Native peoples in western Washington placed Douglas-fir cones near their campfires to ward off wet weather or stop the rain.

Bark, twigs, needles, pitch, and other parts of Douglas-fir trees also found diverse uses as antidotes or treatments for injuries and common health problems. These treatments were typically administered in the form of an infusion or decoction, both prepared by boiling plant parts in water. (Infusions usually entail boiling softer materials, such as leaves or needles, for relatively short periods of time, similar to steeping a cup of tea. Decoctions are prepared from coarser materials like roots, bark, or twigs and boiled for longer periods to recover extracts that are thicker in consistency or more potent.) An extract made from boiling the bark of living Douglas-fir trees was used to treat stomach problems and diarrhea, and a decoction of the twigs was used as a diuretic. An infusion of young shoots and needles was used to treat colds and make tea. Inland Northwest native peoples also chewed Douglas-fir shoot tips as a breath freshener and stuffed the tips of their moccasins with needles to reduce perspiration and prevent athlete's foot. Pitch was used to relieve sore throats, as a cough suppressant, and as a sort of chewing gum. A dressing (poultice) of Douglas-fir pitch was applied directly on cuts, boils, and other skin ailments. Coastal First Peoples mixed pitch with spiny dogfish oil to induce vomiting for relief of intestinal pain and diarrhea, and a mixture of Douglas-fir ashes and animal fat was used to treat rheumatism.

A towering coastal Douglas-fir tree marked the spot of mid-1800 treaty negotiations that dramatically reduced the area of Indian-occupied lands in northwestern Washington and transformed the native way of life. On December 26, 1854, the Medicine Creek Peace Treaty was signed by Washington territorial governor Isaac

Stevens and representatives of the Nisqually, Puyallup, and Steila-coom Indian tribes, among others. The bargaining took place not far from the Medicine Creek Fir, a stately old Douglas-fir named for the nearby creek (since renamed McAllister Creek). Under the treaty, the tribes gave up most of their extensive land holdings, which comprised a significant portion of western Washington, for a mere $32,500. The tree, which blew over in a windstorm more than a century and a half later, far outlasted a way of life that gradually died after the treaty was signed. The fallen tree and the signing site are located within what is now the Billy Frank Jr. Nisqually National Wildlife Refuge at the south end of Puget Sound.

Douglas-fir also featured prominently in some spiritual celebrations and tribal ceremonies. On All Souls' Day, a Christian holiday ultimately celebrated by the Mountain Pima Indians of northern Mexico, celebrants used a mat woven from Douglas-fir branches to cover the graves of deceased relatives. Sometimes in lieu of a mat, a cross-shaped decoration was crafted from smaller branches and twigs and placed at the center of the grave.

Douglas-fir branches and twigs were also an integral part of tribal ceremonies and dance regalia, especially among Southwest Indians. The Hopi people historically occupied (and still do) the parched country north of the Mogollon Rim in east-central Arizona, a place where infrequent rains were a cherished gift from the spirits, known as *katsinas*. Elaborate ceremonies with prayers and singing were used to implore the katsinas for desperately needed rain. The requests were part of a ceremony involving dancers adorned with small Douglas-fir branches. Because Douglas-fir typically did not grow near the arid ceremony sites, either runners or horseback riders were dispatched to the nearest trees to cut the needed boughs. Larger boughs stuck in the ground served as a metaphor for the Douglas-fir maidens mentioned in one Hopi song:

Tuma ítamu, tuma aa'aa'aa awya
Ayó' tivongyapami'i salavimanatuyu

Itamuy nùutayta sonwakw pitsangwa'ikyango
Put hapi aapiy pòötavilawu, ínamu
Pantaqat ánga'a ítamu ųmumi yooya'ökini

Let us all, let us go there
To the dancing display place where the Douglas-fir maidens
In beauteous countenance, are awaiting us
From them (Douglas-fir maidens), you, our fathers, are laying
    the sacred cornmeal path (toward us)
Along that way (path), we will arrive to you as rain

The earliest use of Douglas-fir in the Southwest is not well documented. Nomadic Paleoindian hunters traversed areas of the Southwest seasonally more than 10,000 years ago, and sporadic opportunistic use of Douglas-fir for fuel likely first occurred at that time. More regular use of the trees for fuel, implements, and pit house corner posts likely didn't occur until about 2000 years ago.

At Grass Mesa Village in southwestern Colorado, the Douglas-fir roofing beams used in construction of the great kiva—an underground structure used for ceremonies and rituals—were estimated to have been placed more than 1200 years ago. Because a thick layer of soil was placed on the kiva roof, ponderosa pine and Douglas-fir were the only tree species in the area that could provide timbers long enough and strong enough to serve as primary beams. Douglas-fir is stronger than ponderosa pine and thus preferred for load-bearing roof beams. However, because the source for Douglas-fir timbers was considerably farther from Grass Mesa Village than ponderosa pine, fewer than 10 percent of the beams were crafted from it.

Douglas-fir timbers also formed the backbone of structures at Walpi Village, a Hopi settlement established in the thirteenth century at First Mesa in northeastern Arizona. After the Pueblo Revolt by the Hopi against the Spaniards in 1680, the village was moved for defensive purposes to a finger ridge extending out from the main mesa. In 2012, Walpi Village was named a World Monuments Fund site, which sparked efforts to begin restoring several houses the following year. Except for the roofs, all the original construction materials for the houses were retained, and the Douglas-fir timbers in the houses were classified relative to their manufacture either before or after the Spanish occupation. It was assumed that the Walpi people lacked the need to produce decorative timbers prior to the Spaniards' arrival; hence, the more modest timbers were designated as Walpi in origin, and the fancy or decorated timbers were assumed to be of Spanish design.

I n the Pacific Northwest, early Euro-American arrivals were universally awed by the size and potential utility of the Douglas-fir forests they encountered. British explorer James Cook may have been the first to capitalize on the size and strength of coastal Douglas-fir timbers. In 1778, Captain Cook and his two-ship fleet were working their way along the northern Pacific Coast. A brief onshore reconnaissance of Vancouver Island revealed forests dominated by massive, clean-boled Douglas-fir trees. Unable to resist, Cook replaced the spars on his ships, the *Resolution* and *Discovery*, with new ones made from Douglas-fir.

Decades later, Douglas-fir would become the species of choice on the high seas; one captain even boasted that Douglas-fir spars could be had for the cutting along the Northwest Coast. This news piqued the interest of the Royal Navy, which had long sought a dependable supply of spars to service its far-flung fleet. In the latter 1700s, it had brazenly applied the king's insignia on potential white pine spar trees growing on private lands in the northeastern United States. This action irritated New England colonists who regarded it as a "taking" of an important resource by the Crown, and was just one more factor contributing to the Revolutionary War.

In the 1840s, the Royal Navy located a prime parcel of old-growth Douglas-fir on Vancouver Island and drew up a contract with a local businessman to manufacture one hundred spars by 1850. No spars were delivered, and the contract had to be extended repeatedly. The project was hindered by repeated raids of ships by local native peoples and the threat of injury or death to sailors who came ashore. Another obstacle was how to get the massive spars from the stump to the ship and, once the spars were loaded, how to transport them on vessels designed for general cargo. Meanwhile, as the Royal Navy's military forays diminished, so did their appetite for spars.

Demand for spars had also emerged elsewhere. In 1855, Pope and Talbot's Puget Mill sent a cargo of Douglas-fir spars for sailing ships worth $350 each (equivalent to nearly $11,000 each in today's dollars) to Valparaíso, Chile. The entire Spanish navy was also equipped with Douglas-fir spars from Puget Sound. Some 3500 spars were shipped from Vancouver Island to Australia, England, and Latin America during the heyday of the 1860s, purportedly making the spar trade more profitable than opium at the time. But in the years that followed, despite an occasional shipment of smaller spars, the initial promise of a thriving Douglas-fir spar industry along the Pacific Northwest Coast sputtered and died.

However, the spar story did not end there. The preference for Douglas-fir spars extended to recreational pursuits as well. A 1901 journal article from India shows they were prized for smaller craft as well: "The Douglas-fir of Oregon is likely ever to remain the favorite wood for use in the racing spars of yachts of the larger class." Even today, one can find Douglas-fir spars for small sailing craft on Craigslist.

Inland Douglas-fir was also favored by pioneers for building cabins and houses of worship across much of the Great Basin and Intermountain West. The first homesteaders had to deal with bone-chilling cold waves and relentless wind, and they were far removed from conventional sources of fuel and construction material. Douglas-fir was often the only timber tree conveniently growing in the mountains near settlements in high-desert valleys. They relied on it for firewood, fence posts, rails, timbers, and framing lumber. An ample supply of firewood was a necessity since old-time cabins and

Mormon pioneers harvested inland Douglas-fir from the Wasatch Mountains to construct the massive dome of the Mormon Tabernacle in Salt Lake City, Utah, in the 1860s. The enormous dome was built using a lattice truss system held together with wooden dowels and wedges. (Courtesy of the Church History Library, The Church of Jesus Christ of Latter-day Saints)

houses had essentially no insulation, with many an occupant complaining that the wind blew right through them.

Small local sawmillers skidded the available Douglas-fir down mountainsides with horses and cut it into lumber, often with portable sawmilling equipment. When mill men depleted nearby timber, they hauled their equipment to other locations.

Douglas-fir from the nearby Wasatch Mountains provided the stout timbers that support the stage in the Salt Lake Tabernacle, where the renowned choir and huge pipe organ perform. Built in the 1860s, the architectural marvel also featured a 150-foot-wide domed roof supported by a lattice of Douglas-fir timbers, an estimated 1.5 million board feet in all. A smaller Mormon tabernacle that was built in Manti, Utah, in the 1870s also employed Douglas-fir columns to support its balcony. Douglas-fir provided the only suitable timber accessible to Manti's settlers at the time.

In the dry mountain ranges, widespread nineteenth-century mining operations stripped off nearly all the trees for use in buildings, mineshaft supports, towers, the heating and smelting of fuel, and flumes for transporting water and wood. Miners also cut huge volumes of inland Douglas-fir for their beehive-shaped charcoal kilns, which they used to extract lead and silver from stony ore.

In 1881, a wrangler searching for lost horses in the Beaverhead Mountains of Idaho noticed lead ore in the roots of an upturned tree. By 1883, the Viola Mining Company had moved in to smelt the high-quality ore, and sixteen charcoal kilns were constructed at the mouth of nearby Coal Kiln Canyon. Charcoal was needed for smelting because it burns hotter, cleaner, and more evenly than wood. Douglas-fir logs were bucked into 4-foot lengths and packed tight into the 20-foot-high kilns. Each kiln required thirty to forty cords of wood per two-day burning cycle and produced about 2500 cubic feet of charcoal, roughly enough to fill a semitruck trailer two-thirds full. Tinder at the bottom was ignited, loading doors were sealed, and vents in the base were regulated to achieve the desired slow burn. In the kiln, as moisture, noncombustible gases, and tars were removed, the wood was reduced to carbon with half its former volume and one-quarter of its former weight. The kiln master watched the smoke color to determine when the wood had been reduced to charcoal.

The sixteen kilns used 75,000 cords of wood annually over the next five years. (A cord contains about 128 cubic feet of wood, commonly measured as 4 feet high, 4 feet wide, and 8 feet long.) Loggers denuded huge swaths of Douglas-fir forest in the nearby Lemhi Mountains to keep the kilns fed. After several highly profitable years, the Coal Kiln Canyon smelter shut down in 1890 due to a combination of the ore running out and lead prices collapsing. Termination of the smelting operation must have caught the kiln operator by surprise—an astonishing 40 acres of neatly stacked, 4-foot-long

To extract lead and silver from ore, miners burned huge volumes of inland Douglas-firs in these charcoal kilns in Birch Creek valley, which is now an interpretive site near Leadore in eastern Idaho. (Historic American Buildings Survey, Library of Congress, Prints & Photographs Division, HAER ID, 30-LEDO.V, 1–7)

Douglas-fir cordwood was left behind. Because of the remote location, the owner was unable to even give the prime firewood away.

Visitors can see historical charcoal kilns that burned primarily inland Douglas-fir in the desert valleys at Birch Creek near Leadore in eastern Idaho (see A Visitor's Guide to Notable Douglas-Firs for details on visiting this site), at Canyon Creek near Melrose in southwestern Montana, and at the ghost town of Piedmont in southwestern Wyoming. Farther south, charcoal kilns largely burned nearby pinyon pine and juniper, but in the high desert north of Utah, Douglas-Fir provided the closest abundant fuel. Moreover, Douglas-Fir was the best wood for charcoaling because of its high density and large trunks. Lower-density lodgepole pine was substituted where necessary, but it also had to be hauled from farther away in the high mountains.

Though the century-long love affair with Douglas-fir for manu-facturing sailboat spars had leveled off by the late 1800s, a new use for the tall, strong boles emerged. In 1893, the state of Washington's exhibit at the World's Columbian Exposition in Chicago featured a 238-foot-tall Douglas-fir flagpole, the world's tallest at the time. Boosters hoped to ignite a new industry in the state by visually demonstrating Douglas-fir's superiority for flagpoles in terms of height, straightness, and strength. It was an opportunity for Wash-ington to stand out among the states—and stand out it did, as the display proved a veritable magnet for fairgoers. Following the expo-sition, boosters promoted the state's Douglas-firs for use as flag-poles all over the world.

The display of the crowd-pleasing flagpole in Chicago was the first of a several-decades-long competition for flagpole supremacy. But it was Oregon that would launch the next salvo in the flagpole war. Residents of Astoria, Oregon, combed the forests around their town and found a tree worthy of world champion status for display at the 1915 Panama-Pacific International Exposition. A virtually flawless Douglas-fir was felled, floated down the Columbia, and then towed by tugboat to the exposition site in San Francisco. The approximately 250-foot timber was taken to the exposition grounds and sunk 10 feet into a concrete block, leaving a 240-foot flagpole. But the massive flag made specifically for display at the exposition fractured the flagpole, postponing the recognition of a new world champ.

In 1915, a huge Douglas-fir timber was shipped from British Columbia to England as a gift to replace the decaying 159-foot flag-staff at the internationally renowned Kew Gardens. The 18-ton, 220-foot-long replacement pole was the largest individual piece of timber ever unloaded on European soil at the time. It was also the new record flagpole, at least for the next three years.

In October 1918, a ceremony was held at Camp Lewis, Washing-ton, to raise the world's largest flag (60 by 90 feet) on the world's tallest flagpole, a 314-foot Douglas-fir. Ceremony organizers either ignored or were unaware of the debacle in San Francisco a few years earlier; the gigantic flag proved too heavy for the top of the tapered shaft, shattering the flagpole soon after it was unfurled. Several other flagpoles in the 200-to-250-foot range would be erected in the years that followed, but none would ever match the short-lived 314-foot giant at Camp Lewis, ending efforts to fly ever-bigger flags on ever-taller poles. However, Douglas-fir flagpoles remained popular well into the twentieth century because of their many desirable qualities. In 1958, British Columbia again sent a replacement flagpole to Kew Gardens. This one was a 16-ton, 246-foot-long pole, and the log yard foreman raved that the immense flagstaff was so "straight and true . . . [that] one man could easily roll it over."

Use of Douglas-fir for railroad ties also gained traction in the early 1900s, initially in the West. The estimated annual production of Douglas-fir cross-ties in California, Washington, and Oregon shot up to nearly 12.5 million by calendar year 1919. An article in the industry magazine *Railway Age* in 1920 reported that despite initial skepticism, Douglas-fir held its own in head-to-head comparisons with the southern pine railroad ties in favor at the time: "It is doubtful whether any cross-tie timber will give a better account of itself in the track bed than Douglas fir."

Even after huge wildfires ripped through coastal Douglas-fir forests near Tillamook, Oregon, in 1933 and again in 1939, much of the blackened wood left behind was still sound. Using Douglas-fir timber sourced from the burned forests, the US Navy constructed two huge blimp hangars at the nearby Tillamook Air Station in 1942. The buildings, named simply Hangar A and Hangar B, became the largest clear-span wood buildings in the world. Hangar A burned in 1992, but Hangar B survived and was repurposed to display historical aircraft and aviation memorabilia. It is now known as the Tillamook Air Museum.

D ouglas-fir's many desirable attributes account for its lofty status as the most economically important tree species in the world. Its wood is strong, stiff, stable in drying, and relatively durable. It can be machined well and is suitable for a very broad range of uses, including its superior application for construction lumber, high-quality boards, and large timbers. Douglas-fir constitutes about one-eighth of all commercial timber volume in the United States, dwarfing the volume of any other species. The World Forestry Center in Portland, Oregon, posits that Douglas-fir provides more forest products than any other tree in the world.

The first plywood ever manufactured from western conifers came about because of a serendipitous series of events in Portland in 1905. Early that year, the city was in a tizzy preparing for a world's fair honoring the centennial of the Lewis and Clark Expedition. Portland Manufacturing Company, a small local firm that crafted wood products, was asked by fair organizers to make something "new and unusual" for a display.

After some head scratching, a co-owner and lathe operator from the company hatched a plan to take three pieces of Douglas-fir veneer and glue them together into a single laminated panel. Using small brushes, they spread animal glue by hand on each piece of veneer. The three-layer Douglas-fir "sandwich" was then placed in an improvised press that used house jacks to ensure the pieces would stick together. The sandwich was left overnight to dry and later trimmed to size, resulting in the first-ever panel of Douglas-fir plywood.

The Lewis and Clark Centennial Exposition opened in June 1905, and Tom Autzen, the seventeen-year-old son of another co-owner, was placed in charge of the plywood exhibit. By October the world's first teenage plywood salesman had shown the panel to tens of thousands of fairgoers. Some would become plywood customers, such as the Nicolai Door Company and Tacoma Fir Door Company. By the late 1920s, Studebaker, Fisher Body, and Seaman Body Company of Detroit began purchasing Douglas-fir plywood for automobile floors and running boards. In just over two decades, tiny Portland Manufacturing's novel fair exhibit had become a multimillion-dollar West Coast enterprise.

Builders praise Douglas-fir lumber because of its high strength-to-weight ratio—better than that of steel. It shrinks and warps so little that in some cases the fresh-cut lumber can be used directly in construction and allowed to dry in place. It also has an excellent performance record when subjected to violent windstorms, earthquakes, and climatic extremes.

Uses of Douglas-fir under extreme conditions in India were featured in a 1916 issue of *The Timbermen*, illustrating this species' versatility and resilience. All woods imported to India in the early 1900s were presumed vulnerable to white ants and unable to withstand the dual climatic extremes of heat and humidity. However, after three years of testing, solid Douglas-fir doors were untouched by ants and unaffected by conditions ranging from 95° Fahrenheit and 90 percent humidity or more to 112°F and very low humidity. Douglas-fir was judged equal in appearance, easier to manufacture, and despite considerable shipping costs, cheaper than teak. It also received accolades when used for drying-room floors in tea gardens. The military used it for shell boxes, and it was also tested for use as street-paving blocks. It was cited as the only timber procurable in India in the lengths needed for bridges or large buildings, and after years of use in Calcutta's brutal tropical climate, Douglas-fir timbers showed no evidence of dry rot.

Until late in the twentieth century, Douglas-fir timber was so abundant and widely available that it was standard material for structural or "dimension" lumber—marketed in 2-inch increments from 2-by-6-inch to 2-by-12-inch boards—as well as thicker posts and beams. However, several factors caused demand for the wood to crater by the 1990s. The supply of large Douglas-fir logs dropped dramatically due to depletion of old-growth timber on industrial and private nonindustrial forestlands, and also because of stringent new restrictions on old-growth harvest on national forestlands. Douglas-fir became an expensive, premium construction lumber alternative and was largely replaced in the mass market by "hem-fir" (mainly western hemlock and various true firs), "SPF" (spruce-pine-true firs), or the even more ambiguously labeled "white wood," all of which are cheaper than Douglas-fir, but inferior in strength, stability, and durability. When these other species are substituted for Douglas-fir, building codes require shorter spans for floor and ceiling joists. These cheaper replacement woods also tend to twist and bow due to heat in some southern US applications. The combination of performance issues with cheaper substitute woods and premium pricing for Douglas-fir joists spurred the development of "engineered wood," including prefabricated roof trusses made of hem-fir or SPF two-by-fours and "I-joists" made of a vertical layer of oriented strand board (OSB, a kind of wafer board) with a narrow, horizontal strip of plywood at top and bottom.

One result of replacing structural Douglas-fir with substitutes was to considerably raise the salvage value of older buildings constructed with high-quality Douglas-fir lumber. For example, when the sports arena at the University of Montana was renovated in the late 1990s, the 2-by-12-inch Douglas-fir bleachers were slated for the landfill. However, local builder and recycling pioneer Steve Loken got word of the bleachers' pending destruction at the eleventh hour and hurriedly obtained permission to salvage them. His crew worked eighteen-hour days to rescue the 1953 vintage planks, salvaging 60,000 linear feet of beautiful old-growth Douglas-fir. Loken has since used the bleachers in several building projects and points out that today, salvaged old-growth Douglas-fir lumber is more valuable than many specialty hardwoods. It is now common practice to rescue old lumber, and markets for it are established in most midsize and larger cities. In the West, Douglas-fir is the primary reclaimed lumber.

In addition to its superior strength, Douglas-fir wood has the highest measure of stiffness (modulus of elasticity) of any North American softwood species, which means it is extraordinarily rigid and can handle a heavy load with minimal bending—all beneficial from a performance standpoint. It is not surprising, then, that vertical-grain Douglas-fir makes attractive and durable flooring. Some interior West entrepreneurs manufacture flooring from slow-growing, sapling- and pole-size Douglas-firs thinned from dense stands and from dead standing firs. In both cases annual growth has been slow, and the narrow rings are composed largely of hard, dark summer wood. Attractive, high-quality Douglas-fir flooring is produced from trees that otherwise have little commercial value and whose removal benefits the health of remaining trees.

In the semi-arid West, where irrigation water has been transported in wooden flumes since the mid-1800s, strong 1-inch-thick, rough-cut (unplaned) Douglas-fir boards have long been the flume-building lumber of choice because they shrink and expand minimally under changing moisture conditions and are less prone to rot than most other inland timber species. Douglas-fir wood is also used for boats and aircraft, where stability is critical despite changes in moisture and temperature.

Rough-cut Douglas-fir is the bread and butter of countless tiny sawmills, mostly one-to-five-man operations dispersed widely across the West. Rough-cut is generally "full dimension" in that a 2-by-4-inch board is actually close to that size, whereas similarly labeled planed or "finished" lumber is only about 1.4 by 3.4 inches, and therefore weaker. Rough-cut mini-mills provide lumber for flumes as well as posts, beams, and other structural wood widely used on farms, ranches, and rustic homes and cabins, as well as upscale lodges and mansions. These mills also custom-cut boards and timbers to sizes unavailable at conventional lumberyards. "Circle-sawn" Douglas-fir features the shallow curved incisions of the saw blade. It is produced by small mills and has become fashionable for flooring and appearance wood.

A new, innovative use for Douglas-fir has emerged in the form of cross-laminated timber (CLT). Cross-laminated products are made from several layers of boards stacked in alternating directions and glued to make large structural panels, in some cases exceeding 50 feet long and 10 feet wide. Doors and windows can be designed within the panels, which simplifies initial construction and later remodeling. Buildings constructed from CLTs have several significant advantages. They sequester carbon, rather than release it, making them more compatible with a sustainable environment than those made of steel, concrete, or other materials. Testing also shows that fire risks are not high. When burned, wood timbers only char on the outside due to their high density, which forms a protective layer that helps maintain structural integrity. In 2019, a 280-foot-tall all-timber building was completed in Brumunddal, Norway, using cross-laminated panels. Tall, all-timber buildings exist in coastal Northwest cities, and taller ones are being built almost every year. Local Douglas-fir is an ideal material for this application.

The environmental rewards for using wood instead of the traditional concrete and steel are substantial. Lumber and related wood products such as plywood and oriented strand board (OSB) require less energy and have less of an environmental impact in production than concrete, steel, aluminum, or plastic building materials. Greenhouse gas emissions associated with wood-based houses are 20 to 50 percent lower than emissions from comparable houses employing steel- or concrete-based building systems. Building with wood generally results in less waste, and recycling wood uses far less energy and creates less pollution than recycling other building materials. Its strength and stability despite changes in humidity and temperature make Douglas-fir an ideal wood for home and large-building construction.

Douglas-fir has been introduced as a plantation tree for lumber products in other temperate regions of the world, where it is valued for its economic importance and its resilience to weather extremes and potentially to the effects of climate change. Coastal Douglas-fir grows vigorously in the moderate climates of northern Europe, providing a timber resource in a region containing few native conifers. By late in the twentieth century, France, Germany, and the United Kingdom had the largest areas planted to Douglas-fir, nearly 1.3 million acres in all. The first Douglas-firs grown abroad arose from seed sent by David Douglas from the Fort Vancouver, Washington, area to Britain in 1826. The Royal Horticultural Society, his sponsor, distributed that seed among its members, and it was planted successfully in many parks and estates. As trees from early British plantings matured, their seeds were widely used for further plantings. Two Douglas-fir trees planted in 1834 gave rise to about four million planted seedlings. As of 2016, the United Kingdom's tallest tree was reported to be a 224-foot Douglas-fir growing near Ardentinny, Scotland.

During World War I about 1.6 million acres of French forests were destroyed. In the following decades coastal Douglas-fir plantations became increasingly common, and by the 1990s they covered about 820,000 acres in France, far more than any other European country. Farther east, the hardier inland variety of Douglas-fir has proven successful in Lithuania, Estonia, and in the forest-steppe region of southern Russia because of its ability to survive severe winters.

In the Southern Hemisphere, New Zealand supports coastal Douglas-fir plantations covering about 170,000 acres, while Chile, Argentina, and Australia have smaller plantations of this variety. In New Zealand, Douglas-fir doesn't grow at the same phenomenal speed as Monterey pine (*Pinus radiata*), but at higher elevations it exceeds the pine's growth rate. In some areas of New Zealand, Douglas-fir regenerates so well that it spreads into native grasslands and is considered a weed that threatens these habitats. In Australia the species is seldom planted for timber production, but is considered very suitable for shelterbelts because it retains limbs and luxuriant foliage down to ground level.

Douglas-fir has also found its way into some niche products and applications, particularly based on its smell and taste. Foliage of coastal Douglas-fir is especially aromatic. Chemical analysis of its branch tips (current-year buds and foliage) shows the presence of more than twenty different volatile oils. The tips have high concentrations of oils typically found in citrus trees, including citronellol, limonene, pinene, and sabinene, which likely account for their lemony fragrance. Companies that develop and sell natural plant products have taken notice. Open a catalog or website of a botanical products company and you may find Douglas-fir herbal essences or makings for Douglas-fir tea. Such products are not restricted to the Pacific Northwest or even the United States; ethnobotanical companies in France, Germany, and the United Kingdom also market essential oils derived from Douglas-fir.

Hood River, a small community an hour's drive east of Portland, Oregon, is home to a one-of-a-kind product based on the taste of Douglas-fir. Distiller Steve McCarthy tweaked the process for developing his Douglas-fir-based *eau de vie* for years before getting a product that met his expectations. First he had to overcome the general perception of *eau de vie* as an unrefined beverage. McCarthy threw away the recipe book to develop an *eau de vie* with exceptional depth, individuality, and intensity of taste. He uses the spring buds of Douglas-fir twice in the process, once during distillation for taste and again after distillation for color, producing an inviting clear, pale green liquor. McCarthy markets his unique libation as a Tree in a Bottle, explaining that "it took ten years of experimentation to successfully capture the true essence of Oregon's state tree." Eric Asimov, acclaimed wine critic for the *New York Times*, wrote, "The resulting *eau de vie* is a penetrating blast of forest aroma. On the palate it has the herbal, stomach-settling effect of an Italian digestif."

Not only is Douglas-fir exceptionally widespread in western North America, it also has a diverse record of uses by prehistoric, historical, and modern societies that is unequalled. From firewood to flumes, flagpoles to flooring, snowshoes to spars, and liquor to lumber, no other North American tree has filled more needs or niches in the everyday lives of people, both past and present, than Douglas-fir. No doubt still more uses and benefits will develop over time, despite the tree being so common that many assume we already know everything about it.

CHAPTER 6

Different Forests, Different Fires

When a pall of wildfire smoke descended on western Oregon, western Washington, and southwestern British Columbia in the summer of 2017, many residents probably felt that the stifling black fog was a rare aberration, but instead it was a window to the past and to a rapidly emerging future in the domain of coastal Douglas-fir.

The summer of 1895, for example, was a miserably hot, dry summer, with forest fires burning all around western Washington. Smoke filled the air and eyes burned. Mark Twain visited Puget Sound country that August, and an account of his visit to the region paints a picture of this smoky past. Twain, in poor health and broke, was on a lecture tour trying to raise money during the economic depression that had already caused most Northwest banks to fail. Greeted by a newspaperman in Olympia who apologized for the smoke that obscured the scenery, Twain graciously proffered, "I regret to see—I mean to learn—I can't see, of course, for the smoke—that your magnificent forests are being destroyed by fire. As for the smoke, I do not so much mind. I am accustomed to that. I am a perpetual [cigar] smoker myself."

Later Twain was enraged when much of the audience for his lecture in Bellingham, Washington, filed in late, their trolleys having been delayed by forest fires. He then traveled to Vancouver, British

Columbia, where he awaited a ship scheduled to set sail to Australia. The ship ran aground in the smoky haze, delaying his trip by a week.

What Twain experienced would have been relatively common for residents of the Pacific Northwest in the nineteenth century. Before fire suppression became increasingly successful in the 1930s and 1940s, fire had been the dominant natural disturbance regenerating, shaping, and sustaining forests of both the coastal and inland varieties of Douglas-fir, and the region had occasionally filled with smoke in summer.

Increasingly destructive wildfires in the twenty-first century are largely a result of that fire suppression policy. Fire exclusion has led to a denser understory and allowed forest debris to accumulate, and that buildup of living and dead fuels, combined with summer drought—presumably exacerbated by warming temperatures—has made Northwestern forests more and more combustible. Wildfires burn longer and over larger areas than they would if the forests were allowed to burn more frequently, following their natural cycle. In 2017 the record-breaking wildfires in interior British Columbia, a region now commonly plagued by severe wildfires, sent a blanket of smoke southward that settled across the Northwest, with authorities issuing health alerts in the Puget Sound metro areas. East winds also dumped smoke into Portland and the Willamette Valley, Oregon, from fires in the Columbia River Gorge. Still other wind patterns blew smoke westward across the Cascades, and northward from big fires in Douglas-fir forests of southwestern Oregon.

Even though fire exclusion is still largely effective in coastal Douglas-fir forests, uncontrollable wildfires in southwestern Oregon and in interior Douglas-fir forests east of the Cascades and up the Fraser River drainage in British Columbia will likely pour more and more smoke into southwestern British Columbia, western Washington, and western Oregon, creating breathing problems and inconvenience for millions of people. It also seems likely that the trend toward near-record drought and deficient mountain snowfall in the coastal Douglas-fir forests along with a warming climate will soon produce dangerous wildfires in the heavily populated region itself, extending from the Willamette Valley north to southwestern British Columbia.

It is imperative that those who manage forests take a different approach than the policies practiced in the past century, when fire suppression became the norm. The first step is to understand—as native people did—that fire is an integral part of the environment. As one might suspect for such an incredibly wide-ranging and adaptable tree, Douglas-fir's relationship to forest fire is complex and puzzling. The coastal and inland varieties respond to fire in dramatically disparate ways. Coastal Douglas-fir is highly fire-resistant and generally depends on fires to perpetuate it in the face of competition from a host of more shade-tolerant (but less fire-resistant) species that otherwise crowd it out. In inland forests, conversely, Douglas-fir is *more* shade-tolerant than ponderosa pine, its most common associate, seemingly giving it a leg up in the silent war to gain growing space and eventually dominate. Frequent, low-intensity fires historically kept this scenario from playing out by killing most of the fire-vulnerable small Douglas-firs and maintaining the survivors as a negligible component of ponderosa forests.

In years past when conditions were right in the moist coastal Douglas-fir forests, typically during an extreme drought, lightning-ignited fires ripped through thousands of acres of old forest, leaving huge expanses of charred snags with some scattered unburned areas and large, old Douglas-fir survivors in their wake. These intense infernos that swept through areas of Douglas-fir forest at century-long intervals were critical in sustaining magnificent trees over much of the coastal landscape. Old Douglas-fir has thick bark that insulates and protects the cambium (thin layer of growing tissue) from lethal heating in moderate-intensity fires, which often don't destroy its tall canopy. It grows faster than its competitors, and as it matures, lower branches die and fall away, making the tree less susceptible to canopy scorch from a surface fire. These historic fires also consumed much of the thick organic layer covering the ground, leaving a sunlit mineral-soil seedbed favoring Douglas-fir regeneration. The surviving trees dispersed seeds and reproduced on the newly created open ground.

Over centuries, a crazy-quilt pattern of different-aged swaths or patches of Douglas-fir forest developed, ranging from recently burned areas to others in various stages of development, including some ancient forest areas either missed by wildfires or in fire-resistant locations. The kind of forest in the burned areas changed, but the overall mosaic containing patches in different stages of development did not. Without fire, coastal Douglas-fir is crowded out by shade-tolerant competitors that are able to become established under a closed canopy. The fact that the coastal variety was historically the most abundant forest type west of the Cascade Crest testifies to the role fire played in shaping the splendid forests that amazed the first explorers and settlers.

In rain forests on the Olympic Peninsula and the west side of Vancouver Island, where annual precipitation averages 120 to 200 inches, the presence of Douglas-fir indicates that historical intervals between fires lasted three hundred to perhaps five hundred years. If the intervals lasted longer than that, the species would eventually be eliminated. In southwestern Washington and in Oregon, virgin forests dominated by coastal Douglas-fir commonly experienced fire at intervals of less than three hundred years. Presumably "stand-replacing fires"—those that killed most trees of all species—were common. Still, a few large old Douglas-firs probably survived here and there, and their seeds, attached to a papery wing, were likely borne by winds into burned areas, where they germinated in the rich mineral soil. Also, green cones can survive in the tops of tall dying Douglas-fir trees and continue to mature and cast their seeds.

Extensive areas of old-growth coastal Douglas-fir forests are found in national parks and national forests in the coastal mountains and in the Cascades, where most sites receive 100 inches or more of annual precipitation and are much colder than the significantly drier lowlands. These wet mountain forests historically burned at intervals averaging one hundred to five hundred years. Because of fire exclusion, the old-growth forests lack young, post-fire Douglas-fir communities with their rich assortment of fruit-bearing shrubs and succulent herbs. Old-growth areas logged prior to protection under the 1994 Northwest Forest Plan have some similarities to young post-fire communities, but a burned forest differs from one that has been logged in having a wealth of standing dead trees that attract insects, woodpeckers, and other insect-feeding birds. Also, most burned forests experience a surge of native shrubs and herbs that reflects a temporary flush of nutrients to the soil.

A surprising history of fire's interaction with old-growth coastal Douglas-fir forests came to light from an intensive study of fire history on the west slope of the Cascades east of Eugene, Oregon. Annual rainfall here averages a copious 100 inches, but the dry summer period lasts longer than it does farther north. Investigators discovered that historical intervals between fires averaged between 95 and 150 years at a given location and that many of the living Douglas-fir trees predated the fires. They mapped the complex pattern of fire mortality and survival during the nineteenth century in these forests and found that some of the living trees had regenerated soon after the individual fires, which they had dated from ancient fire scars extending as far back as the fifteenth century. The scientists concluded that historic fires were primarily of "mixed severity," killing some patches of Douglas-fir while other patches survived. Presumably more of the competing western hemlocks were killed. Numerous studies have implicated both lightning and people as ignition sources. Some American Indian tribes lit fires on purpose—for instance, to enhance production of useful plants, to create forage that attracted deer, as signal fires, and so forth. However, once fires started, the people had no means of keeping them from spreading far and wide.

In addition to favoring coastal Douglas-fir, fires help sustain a productive forest ecosystem. Mixed-severity and crown fires commonly lead to a sudden upsurge of red and Sitka alders, which capture atmospheric nitrogen and add it to the soil. Then, benefiting from soil enrichment, Douglas-fir saplings grow up rapidly through the alders. Charcoal from burning provides both short- and long-term contributions to nutrient cycling and soil fertility. Burning also releases nitrogen and other nutrients tied up in forest floor litter and organic matter. This flush of nutrients plus the sunny conditions in burned openings ushers in a host of flowering plants and shrubs that provide forage, seeds, and fruits important for wildlife, from songbirds to elk. The profusion of lush forage plants, seed-bearing shrubs, and alder and other short-lived deciduous trees, including mountain-ash (*Sorbus*) and bitter cherry (*Prunus emarginata*), contrasts dramatically with the dearth of forage and fruits in the undergrowth beneath the heavy shade of a mature conifer forest.

Fire cycles also affect soil chemistry, which can in turn influence the development of pathogenic fungi. In the Puget Sound to Willamette Valley region and in southwestern Oregon, forests dominated by coastal Douglas-fir had for millennia burned at relatively short intervals, ranging from almost annually in the Willamette Valley to about every thirty-five years in the Puget Sound area. These disturbances played an integral role in sustaining the natural ecosystem. By the turn of the twenty-first century, absence of fire had resulted in outbreaks of root disease and other pathogens that weakened and killed many of the fifty-to-one-hundred-year-old trees that had regenerated after a series of logging operations that had begun in the late 1800s. The long period of excluding fire and the associated increases in pathogens and vulnerable, shade-tolerant tree species will likely prevent many of these young forests from ever approaching the age and size of their nineteenth-century ancestors.

In Gifford Pinchot's *Breaking New Ground*, he describes the charcoal-rich soil and the new growth he saw flourishing in the openings left by fire on the rainy western side of the Olympic Mountains. His nineteenth-century findings were made in what is now called the Olympic Rain Forest, east of Forks, Washington, the wettest city in the forty-eight contiguous United States:

> But the most significant thing I found, and to me it was an amazing discovery, was that every part of the [Olympic Forest] Reserve I saw appeared to have been cleared by fire within the last few centuries. The mineral soil under the humus, wherever it was about the roots of windfalls, was overlaid by a layer of charcoal and ashes. Continuous stretches of miles without a break were covered with a uniform growth of Douglas fir from 2 to 5 feet in diameter, entirely unscarred by fire. Among them numerous rotting stumps of much larger trees did bear the marks of burning. I did not see a single young seedling of Douglas fir under the forest cover, nor a single opening made by fire which did not contain them.

In contrast, the dry rain-shadow side of the Olympics had a far different Douglas-fir fire history, which also relates to that of the Puget Sound–Willamette Valley region.

The role of fire in inland Douglas-fir is even more variable than that of its coastal kin. In the drier, ponderosa-pine–dominated inland forests, the common co-occurrence of abundant ignition sources, dry air, and ample fine, low-moisture fuels (pine needles, twigs, dead grasses) historically sparked low-intensity surface fires every few years to every few decades, which kept the successful establishment of young Douglas-fir in check. Nowhere is this more evident than on the forested top of the Rincon Mountains, an isolated "island" mountain range that rises 6000 feet above the Sonoran Desert just east of Tucson, Arizona. Numerous surface fires have occurred here since 1900, significantly affecting the composition of this high-elevation forest. Large Douglas-firs dominate the adjacent moist north slope where fires were absent, but firs are completely missing from the relatively flat mountaintop that burned frequently, including from the occasional draws or swales that would be moist enough to support them. The area experienced frequent fire before the 1900s as well, due to a combination of burning by American Indians and lightning.

Fire, whether ignited by lightning or humans, was the dominant disturbance influencing the ever-changing number, age, and arrangement of trees and the ebb and flow of species composition in ponderosa pine–Douglas-fir forests throughout the West. In general, the greater the number of surface fires, the fewer the Douglas-fir. Some smaller, fire-resistant ponderosas survived the frequent fires, but younger Douglas-firs with limbs close to the ground typically torched out and died. Over time, fire relegated Douglas-fir to a minor or negligible presence in these frequently burned inland forests, preventing it from displacing the more fire-resistant pine and its highly resistant companion in the inland Northwest, western larch. The historical mixed forests of this somewhat moister region, characterized by the handsome orange to reddish trunks of pine and larch along with the less conspicuous grayish-trunked Douglas-fir, were mostly open-grown and at low risk to severe fires and epidemics of insects and disease, unlike the vulnerable stands of today.

In the high-desert country, which is too cold for ponderosa and larch, Douglas-fir becomes the most fire-resistant tree by default. Its companions here, including short, bushy limber pine and juniper, and at higher elevations, thin-barked lodgepole pine, are all less fire-resistant. In these and other semi-arid environments, Douglas-fir attains its greatest longevity, four hundred years or more, before succumbing to trunk or root rot or to other pathogens, which often get established in fire scars.

In addition to semi-arid forests, Douglas-fir becomes the most fire-resistant tree in vast high-elevation lodgepole pine forests that stretch from central British Columbia to southern Colorado and characterize most of Yellowstone National Park. Rather than surviving, lodgepole's strategy is to succumb to fire and regenerate profusely from seeds stored in pitch-sealed cones. The cones open with the heat of fire and cast their seeds into the ashy seedbed where there is little competition. In the past, mixed-severity fires killed and regenerated the thin-barked lodgepole pine while mature Douglas-firs insulated by thick, corky bark often survived. Thus, the crowns of centuries-old Douglas-firs that survived past fires project high above the shorter, uniform layer of lodgepole pines, which date back only to the last fire. Hikers plodding through a monotony of 8-to-12-inch-diameter lodgepoles in these forests will notice the 3- or 4-foot-thick trunks of veteran Douglas-firs that survived past fires. Fires today tend to spread from treetop to treetop, and these increasingly prevalent crown fires kill the old Douglas-firs as well.

Retakes of century-old photographs provide us with a glimpse into the unprecedented changes that Yellowstone National Park's old-growth Douglas-firs have undergone as a result of fire. The Douglas-fir communities that cover much of the park's semi-arid northern region, where the high valleys and adjacent uplands receive a paltry 12 to 18 inches of annual precipitation, are in an area called "winter range" because it provides forage for deer, elk, bison, and bighorn sheep during the long, harsh winter season. Tree scars dating back to the early sixteenth century show that fires occurred every twenty to twenty-five years or so. These frequent surface fires maintained open, patchy stands featuring large old Douglas-firs, as shown in early photos. Fires sweeping through dry grass in the open stands and savannas killed many young trees, but some survived an initial fire and grew large enough to develop thick, fire-resistant bark. Some of the old-growth trees in these open stands have visible fire scars, while stumps of similar trees felled outside the park reveal fire scars that were hidden by newer wood and bark. Still other old trees have no fire scars because their bark became thick enough to protect their sap-filled inner bark and the growing tissue from lethal heating, which occurs at about 145° Fahrenheit.

The twentieth-century transformation of Douglas-fir plant communities so strikingly illustrated in Yellowstone Park's Northern Range is a widespread phenomenon in the mountains of the interior West. However, near mining boomtowns that sprang up in the 1860s, the historical pattern of frequent fires in Douglas-fir–grassland communities had already been interrupted for decades before foresters instituted fire suppression. Evidence points to heavy grazing of grass to supply beef to the thousands of people who converged on the mining areas in the Mountain West to seek their fortune and flee the draft and carnage associated with the Civil War.

In more moist, high-elevation forests, Douglas-fir accompanies the far less fire-resistant subalpine fir and Engelmann spruce. But without fire or other disturbance (such as an avalanche or logging) to open up the stand, subalpine fir or spruce crowd out Douglas-fir.

Anthropologists have concluded that American Indian burning practices date back thousands of years, probably since the Northwest's Douglas-fir forests developed after the retreat of ice age glaciers. Native people lit fires for a great variety of purposes, and records of historic fires suggest or provide evidence of their role in burning. Tree rings can be an especially useful source for estimating when fires occurred, the average number of years between fires, the possible sources of ignition, and even the season of burning. A study of fire scars in mixed ponderosa pine–Douglas-fir forests in west-central Montana analyzed the year of burning and whether scar formation occurred in the earlywood (spring) or latewood (summer) portion of the annual growth ring. Scars showed that the historical mean interval between fires for the area was seven years (it ranged from two to fourteen years); surprisingly, about two-thirds of the fires occurred in the early part of the growing season. Lightning storms without accompanying rain seldom occur during the spring in this area of Montana, which implicates American Indians as the likely source of ignition for these early-season fires.

Burning conducted by native people was also a fundamental part of the ecology of coastal Douglas-fir forests. Botanical explorer David Douglas reported some of its purposes based on observations from his 1826 trip through the Willamette Valley:

> Most parts of the country burned; only on little patches in the valleys and on the flats near the low hills that verdure is to be seen. Some of the natives tell me it is done for the purpose of urging the deer to frequent certain parts to feed, which they leave unburned and of course they are easily killed. Others say that it is done in order that they might better find honey and grasshoppers, which both serve as articles of winter food.

The first caravan of pioneers that arrived in the Willamette Valley, at the end of the Oregon Trail, also recognized the importance of intentional burning in cultivating the landscape. The newcomers beheld a land of grassy meadows, Oregon (garry) oak groves, and patches of Douglas-fir, but large parts of the valley had been burned by native people and lacked forage for the pioneers' livestock. George Emmons, a member of the US Government's Wilkes Expedition, wrote one of many accounts of Willamette Valley burning in early August 1841:

> The country becoming smoky from the annual fires of the Indians—who burn the Prairies to dry and partially cook a sunflower seed—which abound throughout this portion of the country & is afterwards collected by them in considerable quantities & kept for their winter's stock of food. The forests are also frequently burnt to aid them in entrapping their game.

Indigenous cultural practices are believed to be the primary cause of the continual burning that maintained the grasslands and oak woodlands for thousands of years. Evidence from studies of layered sediments in lakes and ponds indicates that the Willamette Valley's grasslands and oak woodlands became abundant after the emergence of a warm, dry climate about eight thousand years ago. Despite the onset of a cooler and wetter climate about four thousand years ago, this deliberate burning by tribes limited the invasion of Douglas-firs until the settlers arrived.

Other areas of prairie and oak woodland once occupied western Washington northward past Seattle and in the dry rain shadow of the Olympic Mountains near Sequim and in the San Juan Islands. This vegetation was more extensive in southwestern Washington and became more scattered and linked to favorable soils north of Olympia, where conifer forest covered most of the lowlands. The prairies and oak groves teemed with diverse herbaceous food and forage plants that produce nutritious bulbs or tubers such as camas and bracken fern, and seeds like sunflowers and nuts, including acorns.

These fire-dependent prairies stood in marked contrast to the less useful vegetation beneath the surrounding Douglas-fir forests. Beginning in the 1990s, conservationists and agencies began using prescribed fire, conifer removal, and control of nonnative invaders like Saint John's-wort (*Hypericum perforatum*) and Scotch broom (*Cytisus scoparius*) to restore a few of the remnant oak woodlands and prairies that hadn't been converted to farms or developments. Fort Lewis Prairie, south of Tacoma, Washington, is well known for historical bunchgrass communities and oak groves. Prior to early logging, the surrounding forest was dominated by big, open-grown Douglas-firs accompanied by stout western redcedars in wet sites that survived and benefited from the Indian fires.

The Kitsap Peninsula, in the middle of the Puget Sound basin, was originally dominated by a vast forest of big Douglas-firs, yet the southern part had a scattered "Oak Patch" (no doubt on the shallowest rocky soils), which was an eponym describing the fire-dependent Oregon oak (*Quercus garryana*) openings that have now virtually disappeared. Also, in the 1950s the Kitsap Peninsula's forests still contained big Douglas-fir stumps resulting from nineteenth-century logging. Some of these stumps had char and fire scars dating to a time long before the pioneers and lumbermen arrived. Careful inspection still reveals char on the outer bark of the few old-growth Douglas-firs that escaped logging in the county's Illahee Forest Preserve, especially on the steep slopes heading east and down toward the salt water, as do a handful in neighboring Illahee State Park near Bremerton. There are also some exceptionally large old firs in the Kitsap Forest Theater and Preserve—west of Kitsap Lake in a narrow, secluded valley near the start of the highway to Seabeck—that still retain what is likely char on their outer bark.

A study reported by paleobotanist Estella Leopold, daughter of famous conservationist Aldo Leopold, indicates that lowland Douglas-fir forests in the Puget Sound area burned with low-intensity surface fires about twice a century—probably from a combination of lightning, Indian fires, and settler-caused fires. Forest inventory data in 1907 from King County show that the dominant Douglas-fir trees measuring up to 8 feet in diameter were spaced far apart, 10 to 25 yards. Old-time loggers stated that this forest was easy to walk through and resisted damage in fires that escaped from logging areas or homesteads. The implication was that before fire suppression became established in the early twentieth century, low-intensity fires and the heavy canopy cover associated with huge Douglas-firs suppressed development of the thick understory common in today's forests.

The extensive lowlands lying between the coastal mountains and the Cascades in Oregon and Washington, and stretching north to Vancouver Island's southeastern coast, average only 40 to 50 percent of the annual moisture that the mountains and the ocean strip receive. In summer the interior lowlands often experience long periods of warm, rainless weather and low humidity. By the late nineteenth century, an ever-expanding population of European immigrants and their descendants was concentrated here, starting the escalating trend that makes it the most heavily populated area north of California.

We know that burning by American Indians had a profound influence on the lowland vegetation, but fires set in the prairies, oak savannas, and lowland Douglas-fir forests no doubt often spread into still more forestland. Also, native people were known to burn forests to facilitate travel, stimulate berry production, improve visibility of wild game, and for myriad other purposes, such as signal fires.

Major William Thornton reported two Indian signal fires in his travels through southern Colorado in 1855. Because one of the burns appeared to be approaching his unit, he sent a scouting party to investigate the situation to see if it posed a risk. Similarly, in the spring of 1886, Army Lieutenant John Bigelow and his troops were searching the frequently burned Rincons for Apaches when they received a dispatch from Fort Lowell, near Tucson: "Signal fires have been seen in the Rincon Mountains the last two nights." Bigelow responded, "These signal fires are doubtless the burning woods that have been observable to us ever since we came here." Pre-1900 fires originating from lightning and from American Indian tribes, along with frequent lightning-ignited fires after 1900, inadvertently but effectively kept Douglas-fir from growing in mixture with ponderosa pine in high-elevation areas of the Rincons.

In southwestern Montana and eastern Idaho, inland Douglas-fir makes up much of the forest bordering the high-elevation valleys of sagebrush and grass. W. A. Ferris, who traveled this country extensively as a fur trapper between 1830 and 1835, provided accounts of free-ranging Indian fires, similar to observations made previously by Lewis and Clark. As he and his companions crossed the Continental Divide from today's Montana to Idaho via a high pass, "Cota's Defile," they overlooked the broad Lemhi Valley and saw "a dense cloud of smoke from the plains forty or fifty miles to the southeastward, which we supposed to have been raised by the Flatheads. . . .

The Indians with us answered the signal by firing a quantity of fallen pines."

Ferris described a feeling of "uneasiness as we were now on the borders of the Blackfoot country, and had seen traces of small parties [of them], who it was reasonably inferred might be collected by the smoke, which is their accustomed rallying signal, in sufficient force to attack us."

Later, while traveling in the Bitterroot Valley of west-central Montana, where dense Douglas-fir forests now occupy formerly open ponderosa pine stands, Ferris encountered Indian-set wildfires intended to welcome his trapping and trading party:

> *We continued down [the Bitterroot] river, till evening and halted on it. The [Flathead] Indians with us, announced our arrival in this country by firing the prairies. The flames ran over the neighboring hills with great violence, sweeping all before them, above the surface of the ground except the rocks, and filling the air with clouds of smoke.*

Another area with conclusive evidence of deliberate burning by native people is Northern California. Tribes applied fire to coastal Douglas-fir in the narrow redwood belt and to small grassy meadows. They burned these prairies to prevent invasion by Douglas-fir and to perpetuate grasses and herbs used for food and medicine. Dry lightning storms are uncommon in the coastal fog belt forest, and the prairies are often green and nonflammable during summer. However, American Indians were able to successfully burn the prairies during brief periods when the grass was dried out, such as on sunny autumn afternoons.

Frequent burning also stimulated sprouts of willow and hazel needed for baskets, which were used for harvesting berries, cooking foods, and many other purposes. The fires also stimulated growth of nutritious grass that attracted deer and elk and exposed the animals to hunters. Field notes from 1939 interviews with Yurok elders of northwestern California record that "burning of hazelnut for basketry occurred every two years; burning under the tan oaks to keep the brush down took place every three years; burning for elk feed occurred every fourth or fifth year; burning in the redwoods for brush and downed fuel control occurred every three to five years."

Fire was the primary tool native people used for culturing vegetation to suit their needs, and they readily made use of it. In a 1916 letter, Klamath River Jack, a native of Del Norte County along California's northern border, describes this cultivation practice:

> *Fire burn up old acorn that fall on the ground. Old acorn on the ground have lots of worm; no burn old acorn, no burn old bark, old leaves, bugs and worms come more every year. . . . Indian burn every year just same, so keep all ground clean . . . [so] no worm can stay to eat berry and acorn. Not much on ground to make hot fire so never hurt big trees, where fire burn.*

The native people had little capability of confining their burns to a specific area, so fires set to renew a prairie spread into the surrounding forest. In fact, tree scars show that many mixed redwood and Douglas-fir forests burned frequently in low-intensity fires. Most of the mature redwood and Douglas-fir trees were undamaged, while the associated western hemlocks and other competing trees often died. Today Save the Redwoods League, the National Park Service, and California State Parks all use prescribed fire to restore some of the coastal prairie ecosystems, but they keep the fires from spreading through adjacent redwood–Douglas-fir forests as they once did.

Although Indians had long tended the wild with fire, only a few visionaries among the settlers of the late 1800s and early 1900s understood the important role fire played in sustaining forests and meeting their needs. Forest managers of that time tried mightily to extinguish fire from forests, which ultimately gave rise to monstrously destructive wildfires. In hindsight, it would have been wiser and easier to have learned to accommodate or mimic the natural role of fire by employing some facsimile of "light" or controlled burning advocated by some forest landowners a century ago. By the beginning of the twenty-first century, foresters and scientists studying natural ecosystems in the West recognized that fire is essential in sustaining many of them and is also an irrepressible force of nature. A great many professionals and laypeople now better understand fire's role in the landscape, but human use of fire currently has far more constraints than in times past.

CHAPTER 7

What Future Awaits Douglas–Fir Forests?

Fostering healthy Douglas-fir forests in an uncertain and challenging future requires an understanding of their relationship to soil and site conditions, associated plant and animal species, and key natural disturbances—in other words, to their ecology. *Ecology* is defined as the interrelationships of organisms and their environment, and while *forest restoration* has many different meanings, for the purposes of this book we define it as "ecology-based forestry." Back in 1899 Gifford Pinchot recognized the ecology of the Northwest's forests, although the science of ecology didn't exist back then:

> *The distribution of the red fir [Douglas-fir] in western Washington, where it is by all odds the most valuable commercial tree, is governed... by fire. Had fires been kept out of these forests in the last thousand years the fir... would not be in existence, but would be replaced in all probability by the [western] hemlock, which fills even the densest of the Puget Sound forests with its innumerable seedlings.*

Several other prominent foresters also concluded that Douglas-fir "would have vanished from the Olympic [Peninsula] forests long ago were it not for repeated fire."

It may seem puzzling then that fire suppression was implemented at all, when at least some foresters recognized the role fire played in a healthy Douglas-fir forest. The story of how in the early 1900s foresters and the public widely embraced a crusade to eliminate an indomitable force of nature provides a lesson about the importance of paying attention to nature and the traditional knowledge of local native peoples. The reasons why so many people of that time chose to suppress or eliminate fire are many, but a crucial one largely absolves them of fault: the science of disturbance ecology only matured near the turn of the twenty-first century.

When Gifford Pinchot explored the western forests, he was awestruck by the mammoth coastal Douglas-firs, the mainstay of a thriving timber industry in Washington and Oregon. Though he recognized that fires shaped the forests and perpetuated the valuable trees, his training came from northern Europe, a region that was normally rainy and humid year-round. European foresters were establishing monocultures of fast-growing trees that didn't resemble the native forests, which had disappeared long ago. Much of the land in Europe, including steep mountain slopes, had been denuded for centuries by a growing population of subsistence farmers who worked very small properties. Despite the poor farmers' appeals to authorities, powerful businessmen repeatedly cleared trees in many large areas. These businessmen used their political clout to clear forests to feed smelters that converted wood into charcoal for extracting iron, copper, silver, and other base metals. John Perlin's *A Forest Journey* describes the destruction of forests through history and the associated consequences since the dawn of civilization. Peasants in Europe used up most of the remaining trees for firewood and lumber and also wanted to convert forest to pastureland.

Based on his European training, Pinchot concluded that the West's native forest of valuable fire-dependent (but old) trees should be converted to stands of young, fast-growing trees. He soon initiated management of the vast publicly owned forests in the West that had been neglected by the federal government. There were plenty of reasons for branding fire as an enemy of the forest. By the latter half of the nineteenth century, prospectors and homesteaders had deliberately set a great many fires to clear away the forest, and careless campers, loggers, and railroad trains spewing sparks into heavy slash along their tracks had inadvertently set many more. These fires were often more severe than those ignited by Indians or lightning, with the ones that couldn't be extinguished spreading across the forest and grasslands for weeks or months, burning until autumn rains or snow quelled them. Several catastrophic fires in the Great Lakes states fueled by heavy accumulations of logging slash and wanton carelessness destroyed frontier communities.

On October 8, 1871, the Great Chicago Fire that killed about 300 people was allegedly started by a cow knocking over a lantern in a barn. On the same day a forest fire named for the small frontier community of Peshtigo, Wisconsin, burned 3.78 million acres of forest and villages in Wisconsin and Michigan, and killed about 1500 people. In 1894 the Hinckley Fire in Minnesota killed 418 people. Out in the Douglas-fir region of western Washington and adjacent Oregon, the Yacolt Burn of 1902 killed 38 people. All of these disastrous fires were ignited by careless settlers and loggers and fueled by logging slash. Ironically all of them involved types of forest that for thousands of years before pioneers arrived had burned less severely.

Into this bleak picture stepped the fledgling US Forest Service. The tiny new agency needed a compelling mission in order to grow. Controlling rampant forest fires filled the bill. Following the disastrous Great Idaho Fire of 1910 (often referred to as the Big Burn for the Timothy Egan book about it) that burned about 3 million acres and cost 85 lives, including some inexperienced men picked up from the streets of Spokane, Washington, to fight the blaze, the Forest Service vowed to prevent future conflagrations. In exchange, a parsimonious US Congress essentially offered an open checkbook.

(Oddly, little attention was paid to the 1889 fires that engulfed a much broader region in the greater Northwest and adjacent Canada. But at that time no government agency claimed it could control future fires.)

After 1910, the Forest Service became fixated on eliminating fires. Their efforts were aided greatly when abundant funding and manpower became available through the Civilian Conservation Corps (CCC) and related work programs in the 1930s, and later by aerial firefighting technology and improved training and mobilization. As a result the Forest Service and cooperating agencies gained success in controlling forest fires. However, by the late 1970s dead material on the forest floor and thickets of young trees had built up to hazardous levels, initiating a trend of huge, uncontrollable forest—an escalating trend exacerbated by the emergence of a warmer, more drought-prone climate.

In the 1970s, after seventy-five years of vigorously promoting exclusion of fire, the Forest Service changed course and adopted a policy advocating managed use of fire. They were belatedly following the advice of early-1900s timberland owners in Northern California and eastern Oregon who had tried to convince the agency to test and improve their techniques of "light burning." These timbermen had been employing low-intensity fires to control the buildup of forest fuels and encroachment of fir thickets in valuable ponderosa pine stands.

Back then, in the early part of the century, the Forest Service had countered light-burning advocates by arguing that low-intensity fires would kill most of the saplings, not recognizing that fire had heavily thinned out the excessive numbers of saplings in centuries and millennia gone by. At the time, professional foresters refused to consider the insight of timbermen, naturalists, and native peoples who had experience observing the forest. These people recognized the implications of using fire in the native western forests that were producing magnificent and valuable trees. Some landowners had learned that over countless centuries low-to-moderate-intensity fires ignited by lightning and Indians had helped produce the original open-growing forests of large trees—ponderosa, Jeffrey, and sugar pines, and western larch, as well as Douglas-fir.

It has been several decades since the Forest Service adopted its policy of fire management, and many new barriers have arisen to prevent its implementation. Increasingly dense forest understories and thickets have developed, and the people who own the ever-increasing millions of new homes now situated in and next to this hazardous forest demand government protection.

Ironically, even the 1964 Wilderness Act, which stated that wilderness should be untrammeled (that is, not hampered) by humans, failed to recognize that fire had been an integral part of natural areas for millennia, and as a result natural fires were vigorously suppressed. An array of other environmental legislation passed by Congress in the 1960s and 1970s, such as the Clean Air Act, failed to acknowledge the inevitability of fire and reinforced society's belief that this natural phenomenon should be extinguished.

A lthough the ecology of the West's Douglas-fir forests seems almost infinitely complex, the fundamentals of these ecosystems are understandable. Likewise the labyrinth of societal and political forces influencing management of publicly owned forests can also be reduced to the basics. To begin, it is impossible to return any of the West's coastal or inland Douglas-fir forests to some primeval state, prior to impact by European colonization. Western forests that developed about ten thousand years ago when a warmer climate emerged after the most recent ice age were shaped by fires that spread unfettered across the landscape. Pinpointing an exact time when primeval forest conditions ended is impossible because both American Indian tribes and lightning have ignited forest fires since time immemorial. Indian use of fire on the land, which had been a significant component of natural fire for thousands of years, was greatly reduced when the US and Canadian governments forced native people to relocate on reservations and when tribal populations declined drastically with the introduction of smallpox and other European diseases.

Now, fires have been suppressed for a century and constrained even longer by the effects of logging, grazing, farming, and all sorts of development over large expanses of land. More than a century of interrupted natural fires cannot be re-created, and fire suppression will continue by necessity in most places because the buildup of fuel in forests threatens the developed landscape.

As the nineteenth century progressed, further disruptions to western forest ecosystems were brought on directly and indirectly by trappers, traders, miners, cattlemen, homesteaders, railroads, the US government, and the need to protect newly established towns and cities from fires that had previously roamed the landscape. The government forced Indians to stop burning and to vacate their ancestral lands, and soon afterward railroad trains began throwing off sparks that often ignited fires next to their tracks.

By the mid-twentieth century, most of the West's Douglas-fir forests were out of sync with primeval conditions, which became obvious in overcrowded inland forests that had gone without burning for periods much longer than any pre-1900 intervals between fires. The historically dominant fire-resistant or fire-dependent conifers were being largely displaced by more shade-tolerant Douglas-fir or true firs. Douglas-fir was also starting to crowd out aspen groves, which provide key wildlife habitat. By the late 1900s, old, thick-barked, fire-resistant Douglas-firs were being killed by wildfires in high-elevation lodgepole pine and mixed conifer forests.

The wetter coastal Douglas-fir forests that once went centuries between fires also came to exhibit effects of fire exclusion. Remaining virgin forests now have few young fire-generated Douglas-fir communities, and the historically dominant Douglas-fir is slowly being replaced by shade-tolerant western hemlock, Pacific silver fir (*Abies amabilis*), grand fir, and white fir. Despite this seemingly bleak situation, there are some management alternatives for restoring greater resilience and sustainability in both inland and coastal Douglas-fir forests based on the historical role of fire. However, this "ecology-based forest management" cannot be carried out at any significant scale unless it garners strong public support, and its advocates can only succeed if they understand the public's perception of forests.

Many people think of the West's native forests as representing unspoiled nature in the twenty-first century. Sparked by Earth Day in 1970, this belief prompted a mass migration into western forests as part of a "back to the land" movement. In more recent years this trend has accelerated, and now tens of millions of people live in what foresters and firefighters call the Wildland-Urban Interface (WUI). This greatly expanded suburban zone in and adjacent to once-open forests that burned in low-intensity fires is now jammed with trees and vulnerable to devastating conflagrations.

According to a 2018 study, when uncontrollable fires burn large areas of the WUI, including scores or hundreds of houses, real estate prices drop for only a couple of years, and thereafter nearby forest homesites accelerate in value. But what the researchers and most laypeople fail to recognize is that the value of burned forest property plummets long term. In addition, the researchers' studies of WUI property values do not differentiate forest from brushland, such as California's chaparral and scrub oak *(Quercus berberidifolia)*. Brushland, such as that in the hills of Southern California, resprouts and grows rapidly. It is sought out primarily for its ability to provide screening and privacy.

In contrast, forested WUI attracts new residents because of the beauty of trees. When a forested WUI is destroyed by fire, a new forest takes decades to develop. The fire leaves the homesite's surroundings in ruins. There may be fifty to one hundred heavily charred dead trees per acre that cannot be left standing because of the hazard and jackstrawed mess they soon create. Most of these burned trees must be felled and removed with heavy equipment, which almost invariably leaves unsightly ruts and skid trails in unvegetated soil that usually becomes soft and muddy with fall and winter rain and snow. Removal of treetops, limbs, and small trees involves even more expense and impact, since most of this material will have to be piled and burned or chipped. Many residents of the WUI whose houses were saved while their forest was destroyed have faced the grim prospect of paying thousands of dollars per acre to clean up the dead trees, while also having to choose between two equally unpalatable alternatives: either staying put and living in a devastated forest or trying to sell their property at a fire-sale price.

Most immigrants to the WUI have scant knowledge of ecology and believe that their forest surroundings can and should remain unchanged. Many subscribe to the illusion that their home will be protected by firefighters. They are unwilling to make their house and surrounding forest fire-resistant, despite the educational efforts offered by state extension forestry and fire departments, among others, and incentives offered by federal grants to reduce the cost of hazard-reduction treatments.

The risks of massive property destruction by fires and possible loss of lives in the WUI have preempted normal firefighting priorities. Manpower and equipment are stretched so thin trying to protect hundreds of homes that they are often unable to control new fires or establish holding lines to keep large fires from spreading. Protecting the WUI wreaks havoc on agency budgets and prevents them from carrying out efforts to restore forests or even conduct highly cost-effective treatments to reduce fuels.

Refusal to recognize fire's natural role in forests has led to laws, regulations, and a judicial process that fails to acknowledge that continuing to suppress fire without actively restoring the forest assures ruinous consequences. It has led land management agencies and jurists to invoke the "precautionary principle," which rejects fuel-reduction treatments on public lands because they might cause damage despite the much greater harm caused by doing nothing.

To counteract the conundrum that prevents ecology-based management of fire-dependent Douglas-fir forests, diverse groups of forest advocates and users are working together to learn about the ecology and issues affecting forests throughout the West. In their meetings and field trips to witness forest conditions, they hear from experts in wildlife management, watershed protection, fire management, harvesting and thinning technology, and so forth. Participants come to understand each others' differing concerns and to respect other parties' viewpoints. These collaborative efforts have increased support for restoring the forest.

Dozens of different collaboratives are involved with the West's Douglas-fir–mixed conifer forests. The Blackfoot Challenge, chartered in 1993, is one of the earliest community-based collaborative committees. Its goal is to keep the rural character of western Montana's 1.5-million-acre Blackfoot River Valley and its tributaries intact. One of the collaborative's priorities is to restore mixed Douglas-fir forests to a more sustainable and fire-resistant structure. Private landowners led a mission to encourage, coordinate, and seek funding for practices that conserve and enhance the area's natural resources and rural lifestyles through cooperation among private and corporate landowners, environmental advocates, logging interests, public land managers, and local governments. Methods include promoting conservation easements, which offer tax incentives for landowners who continue traditional uses and give up rights to subdivide.

In several western states, groups with divergent interests have developed principles of forest restoration in collaboration with the US Forest Service. These groups are now applying these principles in restoration projects on the ground. A collaborative in Utah has established guidelines for restoring aspen groves that serve as important habitat for deer, elk, and migratory songbirds. Historically aspen groves were rejuvenated when the trees regenerated after fires, but due to fire suppression they have been losing their vigor and are being invaded by Douglas-fir and other conifers. One method for restoring aspen is to fell the invading conifers and use those dried-out trees as fuel for prescribed burning.

Northeast Washington Forest Vision has implemented two dozen large restoration projects on the Colville National Forest in northeastern Washington to thin dense stands, remove understory Douglas-firs, and apply prescribed fire, providing nearly two hundred jobs as well as wood needed by sawmills, pulp mills, and an electric power plant fueled by chipped logging slash. This collaborative is working to restore mixed old-growth stands of ponderosa pine, larch, and Douglas-fir that were originally perpetuated by fires.

Another example of collaboration is the work being done by the Bureau of Land Management and a variety of cooperators to limit the encroachment of interior Douglas-fir into historical sagebrush-grasslands in southwestern Montana. They first remove thickets of Douglas-fir and even larger trees, which quickly reseed and are often severely infected with dwarf mistletoe (*Arceuthobium*) and other pathogens, and then follow up by conducting prescribed burns. This program reduces the hazard of severe fires and also aids the threatened sage grouse and rapidly declining monarch butterfly, as well as deer, elk, and moose.

Especially in the inland West, restoring Douglas-fir forests presents an economic challenge, because a majority of the trees that need to be removed have little or no value for lumber or other wood products. Traditional timber sales modified to accomplish restoration objectives may not attract bidders. As a remedy, Congress authorized the Forest Service and Bureau of Land Management to employ "stewardship contracts" to help restore federally owned forests. These contracts specify how the tracts of forest will be treated and what other improvements will be made, such as reducing hazardous fuels or replacing culverts to improve fish habitat. They are offered by bid to logging companies and contractors that apply the value of timber and other forest products removed from some of the stands to offset the costs of services the forests are contractually obligated to receive. Congress has continually expanded programs and funding to improve forest conditions on both federal and privately owned forestland, recognizing that these programs are cost-effective approaches to reduce the ever-increasing hazard of severe wildfires.

In 2018, Congress passed a bill creating Good Neighbor Authority (GNA), which allows state forestry agencies to help the Forest Service and other federal agencies designate large areas that will receive treatments to help restore forests to a more sustainable and less hazardous condition. GNA also engages conservationists, hunters, people in the lumber industry, people with livestock interests, and others in the discussion about appropriate management.

I n the coastal Douglas-fir forests west of the Cascades, from west-central Oregon to southwestern British Columbia, prescribed burning is generally prohibited due to air quality concerns. Upwards of eleven million people live in the Puget Sound trough, Willamette Valley, and associated lowlands, including metropolitan Vancouver and Victoria, British Columbia. Most of this area originally supported an old-growth Douglas-fir ecosystem (see chapter 2) that was perpetuated by periodic burning. Now the coastal mountain ranges to the west and the Cascades to the east trap pollution from automobiles and industries in the lowlands, and potentially smoke from prescribed burning or wildfires.

The 1994 Northwest Forest Plan issued directives for maintaining critical habitat for threatened species such as the northern spotted owl on federal lands in coastal Douglas-fir and related forests, primarily those west of the Cascade Crest. This policy shift brought about a revolution in the way national forests and other federal lands are managed. Instead of clearcutting old forests and establishing plantations to produce young, fast-growing tree crops, foresters gradually shifted to ecology-based management as exemplified by

Variable Retention Harvesting (VRH), which perpetuates characteristics of the different-aged mosaic that once typified most northern coastal Douglas-fir forests.

VRH retains components of the existing stands critical for forest sustainability and endangered wildlife habitat, including old-growth Douglas-firs that historically survived fires, standing snags, and large rotten logs. It retains about one-third of the original live trees but also creates openings favoring vibrant understories and regeneration of young Douglas-firs. Under Professor Jerry Franklin's leadership, VRH has evolved into a comprehensive, ecology-based management system that mimics the natural ecosystem.

One concern is that at a landscape or regional scale, the singular focus on retaining old growth under the Northwest Forest Plan has resulted in a deficiency of the earliest stage of vegetational development, known as the "early seral" stage. Early seral conditions (vigorous and diverse understory plant communities) are estimated to have comprised nearly 20 percent of Oregon's coastal old-growth Douglas-fir forests historically. At the start of the twenty-first century, the early seral stage occupied only about 2 percent of the area. As the VRH concept matures, land managers will have to decide what areas of the landscape and how much of it to treat. Managers of some state-owned timberlands west of the Cascades also apply characteristics of this concept in conjunction with their legislative mandate to produce income for public schools and roads.

One section of western Washington stands out because fire is sometimes allowed to play its natural role there, benefiting coastal Douglas-fir and fire-dependent shrubs and herbs that help maintain biological diversity. Olympic National Park is a secluded enclave amid the 3-million-acre Olympic Peninsula. A maze of rugged mountains incised with deep canyons and valleys, the park is surrounded by national forest, tribal lands, and state forestlands that together occupy most of the lightly populated peninsula. Fortuitously, most of the peninsula's residents live near the windy Strait of Juan de Fuca, which is characterized by good atmospheric circulation. The park's large area and geographical isolation afford it the rare ability to host a limited amount of natural fire and even at times a prescribed fire in the park's western valleys when weather forecasts predict good smoke dispersion.

The Klamath region of southwestern Oregon and northwestern California provides another example in the use of prescribed burning. The Klamath Mountains, prone to severe summer drought and dry lightning storms, are covered with crowded stands of young Douglas-firs and other conifers along with extensive brush-fields that feature highly combustible evergreen shrubs permeated with volatile oils, including juniper, buckbrush, chinquapin (*Castanopsis chrysophylla*), and manzanita (*Arctostaphylos patula*). Thus, since the 1980s, the region has been plagued by huge wildfires. The region's sparse population is mostly located in deep valleys and canyons where a thick pall from wildfires creates temperature inversions that trap dangerous concentrations of smoke for long periods, sometimes forcing residents to evacuate. Uncontrollable conflagrations pose a direct threat to homes and businesses and bring about an expansion of brush-fields into terrain originally occupied by forest. In view of these hazards, local collaborative groups have established strategies of prescribed burning and tree thinning that reduce the threats to people and the ecosystem.

To increase the sustainability of drier inland forests with Douglas-fir, ecology-based management involves treatments aimed at significantly reducing the density of the trees. Treatment plans define a "desired future condition" that makes the greatest headway toward long-term sustainability, given threats from wildfire, insects, disease, and a changing climate. Land managers describe this desired condition in terms of the size, number, species, and general arrangement of the trees. Reconstructions of historically sustainable, old-growth-stand conditions along with results from long-term forestry research serve as useful guidelines for developing treatment prescriptions. Because it is more prone to damage or mortality from root rot, defoliators, and fire than its more shade-intolerant associates on drier sites, hardly any Douglas-firs are retained as long as there are other tree species growing in the area. In contrast, when Douglas-fir occurs in moister mixed conifer stands with more shade-tolerant associates, it is typically retained.

Ecology-based forestry has also been applied to many forests supporting inland Douglas-fir in the vast area east of the Cascade Crest and British Columbia's Coast Range, where enormous wildfires are now common. These wildfires have forced many residents to recognize that fire plays a vital role in their forests, which has spurred support for thinning, fuel-reduction treatments, and prescribed burning. These residents back measures to promote and ensure fire-safe homesites; many of them also favor allowing some natural fires to burn in large wilderness areas.

Despite growing awareness of the need for some form of management intervention, the economic and social benefits of expanding ecology-based forestry in inland Douglas-fir forests are largely overlooked. Fire-threatened and burned-out homeowners experience massive costs and prolonged, elevated levels of stress. Removing excess small and medium-size trees before they burn in a wildfire creates good jobs in harvesting, transporting, and milling, and provides useful products such as lumber, pulp wood, and even chipped branches and foliage for high-efficiency heating systems and generation of electricity. This win-win activity uses a waste product that can be a hazard if left in the woods and reduces the need for alternative materials like steel, plastic, and concrete, whose production and use have a far greater impact on the environment. It also reduces use of fossil fuels and helps create forest ecosystems similar to those that were sustainable by various forms of fire for thousands of years—ecosystems that produced the big Douglas-fir trees extolled by Northwest lumbermen and valued by Rocky Mountain homesteaders.

ACKNOWLEDGMENTS

It is impossible to recall all the people who helped us create this book, but some of the most obvious include Stephen Arno's mentors: Jim Habeck, professor of plant ecology; Bob Pfister, professor of forest ecology; and Jim Brown, fire scientist. Valuable sources of information for Carl Fiedler include David Charlet, professor of biology; Chris Earle, conifers.org founder and webmaster; Don Hanley, forest management extension specialist; Jim Malusa, plant geography scientist; and Doug Page, national forest silviculturist. We are also indebted to ecologist Jerry Franklin for his groundbreaking work on coastal Douglas-fir. Although it is unusual to include our editor, we received outstanding guidance in developing this book from Mountaineers Books editor in chief Kate Rogers.

The three-story lobby at the heart of modern-day Glacier Park Lodge is framed by 40-foot Douglas-fir columns with their bark intact. Its design was inspired by that of the Forestry Building constructed for the Lewis and Clark Centennial Exposition in Portland, Oregon, in 1905. (Glacier National Park Archives)

A VISITOR'S GUIDE TO NOTABLE DOUGLAS-FIRS

Exceptional individual trees and remnants of pre-European Douglas-fir forests still exist in a number of accessible areas across the West. We describe numerous places worth visiting, along with some remarkable trees and unusual features in Douglas-fir forests. Make sure to inquire locally before visiting any of the hard-to-find individual sites or traveling during winter.

CANADA

 Alberta's Inland Douglas-Fir
Waterton National Park North to Jasper Townsite

Douglas-fir grows primarily at low elevations along the eastern edge of the Canadian Rockies from Waterton Park northward. It is still fairly common on warm, dry sites near Banff townsite but decreases northward from there. In Alberta, the northernmost significant outposts of Douglas-fir are groves adjacent to the Jasper townsite in Jasper National Park, about 300 miles northwest of the US border and Montana's Rocky Mountain Front, where, paradoxically, Douglas-fir is very common across a broad range of elevations. The open Douglas-fir grassland near Jasper townsite occupies an unusually warm, dry rain-shadow setting; this area is sought out by deer, elk, and other wildlife during winter as a sanctuary from the surrounding snowy and frigid mountains.

British Columbia's Coastal Douglas-Fir

Belcarra Regional Park: Record-Breaking Tree House

In 1973, nineteen-year-old George Dyson decided to build a tree house. Most children get over their itch for a tree house well before their teenage years, but for Dyson this would be a place to live, not a plaything. He chose a towering coastal Douglas-fir just off the shore of Burrard Inlet and just east of metropolitan Vancouver. Although the tree was located on crown land in Belcarra Regional Park, it was the perfect spot for the young Dyson to follow his dream of designing and building kayaks. Perhaps because he constructed kayaks on the beach directly in front of his home, few people made the connection (or cared) that the tree was on public land within the park.

Captivated by the same stunning scenery that had spurred a Spanish explorer to write of this place in 1792 that "it would be impossible to find a more delightful view," Dyson chose to build his new Douglas-fir home nearly 100 feet above the ground. This lofty perch ensured that his view would remain unobstructed and his home relatively unnoticed. Complete with a cot, writing desk, wood-burning stove, and a couple of salvaged windows, Dyson's home cost him a mere $12 to build. To ensure its safety in high winds, he lashed his finished dwelling to fourteen live Douglas-fir branches using stout nylon twine.

Dyson lived at his elevated Douglas-fir address for three years, in what is believed to be the highest permanently occupied tree house on record. His tree house is described in more detail in a book about him and his father Freeman Dyson, *The Starship and the Canoe* by Kenneth Brower. The remnants of the structure can still be seen from just the right vantage point along the Admiralty Point Trail in Belcarra Regional Park.

Trees modified in the past for human use—whether by bark-peeling, bending, girdling, or horizontal scarring—are referred to as culturally modified trees (CMTs). Native people modified trees to point directions, conduct healing ceremonies, harvest inner bark for food (although Douglas-fir was considered unpalatable), construct canoes, build shelters, or provide fuel for cooking or heating. Most CMTs were modified in the 1800s or before.

Likely the most recent large-scale cultural modification of trees occurred in the 1940s and 1950s on Bentinck Island, located just south of Vancouver Island. In 1924 the Canadian government moved lepers from a colony on D'Arcy Island to a more modern "leprosarium" on Bentinck Island. The Bentinck colony consisted of living quarters, gardens, a piggery, and a cemetery.

At its maximum, twenty-two lepers lived on Bentinck Island. Each resident had their own small cottage with a woodstove, toilet, and running water. It is surmised that the easiest firewood to collect—such as pieces of dead wood or branches on the ground—was gathered during the first couple of decades after the leprosarium was established, and then residents turned to peeling bark for fuel.

A comprehensive tree inventory taken in the 2000s found seventy-three Douglas-fir CMTs in the area surrounding the cottages, with CMTs averaging about 40 inches in diameter. Nearly all CMTs had irregular, approximately rectangular-shaped sections of bark peeled from the lower portion of their boles. The size of the removed bark pieces was typically 1 to 2 feet wide and 4 to 5 feet long. Bark removal scars typically extended from near ground level to head height. Detailed examination of the peeled trees shows that the bark sections were removed using metal tools between 1943 and 1957. It is probably more than coincidence that the beginning of this fourteen-year period coincides with a time when firewood was increasingly hard to find after twenty years of occupation at

A VISITOR'S GUIDE TO NOTABLE DOUGLAS-FIRS

Bentinck, and the end coincides with the death of the last leper in 1957 and the closing of the leprosarium.

Some remnants of the colony can still be found, and most of the Douglas-fir CMTs were reportedly still alive as of 2008. Those interested in visiting the site should first inquire with local authorities, as Bentinck Island has been repurposed as a Royal Canadian Navy test site. The island is located just off Rocky Point at the southern tip of Vancouver Island—separated by a narrow channel known as Eemdyk Passage.

 Capilano Suspension Bridge Park: Treetops Adventure

The Capilano River and surrounding Douglas-fir rain forest have been natural attractions for Vancouver-area residents for well over a century. In 1889, Vancouver's park commissioner, a Scottish civil engineer named George Mackay, foresaw the opportunity to create a unique, top-down view of the Douglas-fir forest and the river that runs through it. Mackay's initial effort was a simply designed suspension bridge constructed using hemp ropes and cedar-plank decking. The bridge was a hit among locals and has changed hands and been rebuilt numerous times since.

The Capilano Bridge complex currently offers an integrated experience blending nature, history, and culture, including the largest private collection of totem poles in the world. Mackay's once-simple suspension bridge has been transformed into a network of seven interconnected bridges and viewing decks called Treetops Adventure. The suspension bridges are anchored to eight 250-year-old Douglas-firs using a distinctive, adjustable tree-collar system that accommodates continuous tree growth without damaging the trees; there aren't any nails or bolts penetrating them. The collective experience affords visitors unparalleled views and perspectives of an old-growth Douglas-fir rain forest from mid-canopy vantage points up to 110 feet above the ground.

Capilano Suspension Bridge Park is located in North Vancouver about a mile north of the Trans-Canada Highway (Highway 1). An admission fee is charged, and guided tours are offered daily.

Cathedral Grove

Cathedral Grove is an outstanding forest of massive Douglas-firs on Vancouver Island, located in 335-acre MacMillan Provincial Park, which straddles Highway 4 on the way to Port Alberni. Trails on the south side of the highway soon take visitors away from traffic noise into a realm of giant Douglas-firs, some more than eight hundred years old, including a tree whose pillar-like trunk is 9 feet thick. Trails on the north side of the highway lead into groves of ancient western redcedars, some of which have scars from bark-peeling by Indians likely made over a century ago. (Cedar bark was traditionally used to make rain-resistant hats, among other items, and shredded for diapers.)

Access to this very popular park is located near the Cameron River bridge at the west end of Cameron Lake. Roadside parking is limited, so it may be best to visit on weekdays.

Hawaiian War Canoe

This account about carving a gigantic Douglas-fir canoe illustrates the vast range of products that have been crafted from this versatile species. The end product is not a destination for visitors as such, although the occasional canoe-building aficionado may be able to arrange a viewing of either the large or small hull.

Historically, native Hawaiians preferred to build their traditional war canoes from Douglas-fir. Since the species was not native to the islands, they used Douglas-fir driftwood that sporadically washed ashore to craft their distinctive double-hulled canoes. In the mid-1900s, controversial anthropologist Thor Heyerdahl theorized that the Hawaiian Islands were originally populated by Indians who had traveled in similar double-hulled canoes from British Columbia's Pacific Coast. Intrigued by the question of whether such a voyage was plausible, Canadian adventurer Geordie Tocher carved a canoe from a single log based on traditional Haida Indian designs. The Haida, whose traditional territory includes islands off the west coast of British Columbia, are renowned for their colorful, seagoing canoes, which were traditionally built from cedar.

In 1971, the intrepid Tocher set out from Vancouver, British Columbia, in his 50-foot canoe, the *Orenda,* bound for Hawaii. Three weeks into the voyage his cedar canoe shattered on a reef off the northern coast of California. Undaunted, Tocher embarked on a second round of canoe-building, this time using stronger Douglas-fir. Fortuitously, the city of West Vancouver offered him a 9-foot-diameter, nearly 300-foot-tall Douglas-fir tree that had been felled in a local park. Tocher painstakingly chopped and chiseled the huge tree and gradually transformed it into a 40-foot-long, 6-foot-wide canoe, the *Orenda II.* A much smaller, 15-foot-long dugout canoe that Tocher had built earlier was used for the second (outrigger) hull.

After enticing two companions to join him, Tocher embarked from Vancouver in the spring of 1978. Using navigation and a sail attached to the outrigger hull, they followed the "natural flotation path of logs and the winds" to Hawaii. Despite encountering up to 35-foot waves, Tocher and his mates completed the grueling 4500-mile journey from Vancouver to Waikiki ahead of schedule, providing evidence that Douglas-fir driftwood or double-hulled Indian canoes could have made their way along Pacific currents from British Columbia to Hawaii.

Upon his return, Tocher made numerous public presentations documenting his incredible voyage but chose not to put his Douglas-fir canoe on display. He subscribed to a Haida custom that "when a vessel has finished its useful life, it should be allowed to return to the elements." To hasten the natural recycling process, he sailed the canoe about 50 miles northwest of Vancouver and left it at the east end of Gunboat Bay. The adjacent Malaspina Ranch agreed to keep it on their property until it has gone back to the soil. The smaller hull is stored at archivist Bas Collins's private museum in West Vancouver.

 ## *Stanley Park*

Stanley Park is a famous historical forest encompassing a 1000-acre peninsula bordered on one side by the city of Vancouver's busy harbor and adjacent to the downtown area. Numerous trails thread through this enclave of old-growth coastal Douglas-fir forest in western Canada's largest metropolitan area. Trail brochures are available at the park entrance and online.

 ## **British Columbia's Inland Douglas-Fir**
Cariboo-Chilcotin: Douglas-Fir Grasslands

Highway 97 heading north to Williams Lake in central British Columbia and Highway 20 branching off westward to Riske Creek (32 miles) and points beyond slice through the expansive semi-arid Cariboo-Chilcotin region. British Columbia's towering Coast Mountains capture nearly all the moisture from North Pacific storms, which helps create a sprawling, picturesque landscape of canyon and foothill country covered with dry grasslands and patches of inland Douglas-fir.

 ## *Fraser River Canyon: Douglas-Fir Manna*

Indians of the Pacific Northwest historically relied heavily on diets of fish, wild game, tubers, nuts, and berries. Some native peoples in the interior Northwest also peeled bark from mature ponderosa pine and harvested the sweet inner bark, or cambium. The cambium was one of the few sweet foods in their diet, and it was also high in vitamin C and antioxidants. However, it was only available for a few weeks each spring and required hard physical labor to harvest. A less well-known but much easier sweetener to gather was found in localized areas of interior British Columbia. A very rare type of sugar, called manna, occurs as frost-like grains encrusting Douglas-fir branchlets, most commonly on trees growing in the Thompson and Fraser River valleys.

Interior Douglas-fir is the only tree in the world that produces this manna, and droughty summers appear especially conducive to its formation. Analysis of the naturally occurring substance yields about 50 percent pure crystalline melezitose, a rare trisaccharide sugar. Scientists who reported their findings in a 1920 issue of *Scientific American* were amazed that Douglas-fir manna went unnoticed by Euro-American explorers and settlers for nearly a century, even though Indians used it as a sweetener during the same period.

Travelers interested in seeing manna firsthand are most likely to find it during warm, dry summers and on Douglas-firs growing in sunny locations along Highway 12 between Lytton and Lillooet, British Columbia.

UNITED STATES

 Arizona's Inland Douglas-Fir
Mount Graham: Mother of the Forest

The nickname Mother of the Forest is likely to inspire visions of a towering centuries-old coastal Douglas-fir growing in a lush rain forest environment, with a clear bole barely tapering to the first branches far above the ground. Who would guess that Mother of the Forest was instead an inland Douglas-fir found at nearly 10,000 feet in elevation in the Pinaleño Mountains of southeastern Arizona?

With huge, coarse limbs up to 2 feet in diameter and growing within 10 feet of the ground, this most unusual tree's asymmetric branches resembled those of an ancient Southern live oak (*Quercus virginiana*) far more than a conifer. Sadly, this charismatic giant was killed by the Clark Peak wildfire in 1996. The charred tree has since fallen, and the huge blackened bole and its massive limbs are slowly decomposing.

Several other wildfires since 2000 have killed most of the remaining large, old Douglas-firs scattered around Mount Graham, most in the 3-to-4-foot-diameter range. In addition, most of a refugium that was specifically reserved as protected habitat for the endangered Mount Graham red squirrel burned in the 2017 Frye wildfire. Wildfires are an existential threat to the squirrels, which feed heavily on Douglas-fir seeds if available, and often cache fir cones near the base of trees where they live.

 Mount Lemmon

Big, tall Douglas-firs thrive in sheltered sites on some of the highest peaks in southern Arizona. Tree enthusiasts will marvel at the 3-to-4-foot-thick Douglas-firs more than 120 feet tall growing on a steep, shady slope near 9000 feet in elevation just below the summit of Mount Lemmon. Tucson's beloved peak is an awesome massif jutting 7000 feet above the sprawling Sonoran Desert. The heavily traveled Mount Lemmon Highway climbs steadily up through desert and semi-desert vegetation and hardy ponderosa pines that reach the 8000-foot level. Nearing the summit, a locked gate closes the final 1.5-mile stretch of highway to motorized use by the public to protect an array of multimillion-dollar telescopes and microwave facilities on top. The gate is adjacent to the small ski resort's parking lot. Hikers can ascend the final stretch of highway, and about a mile above the gate, encounter towering Douglas-firs rooted in a steep ravine immediately below the road. Some of these old-growth trees were killed by a 2003 wildfire that spread high up on the mountain, but most of them survived.

California's Coastal Douglas-Fir
Redwood and Douglas-Fir Forest

Only the coastal variety of Douglas-fir grows in California, although, oddly, low coastal mountains in the far southern part of the state support small populations of the Western Hemisphere's only other species of Douglas-fir, a small tree named bigcone Douglas-fir (*Pseudotsuga macrocarpa*).

Big old coastal Douglas-firs, which often go unnoticed among the redwoods, are something new to look for among their famous companions. Along with California's sequoias, redwoods are the worldwide goliaths among trees. Douglas-firs 7 feet in diameter or more and 275 feet tall are common companions in much of Jedediah Smith Redwoods State Park and Redwood National Park along California's far northern coast near Crescent City and Eureka. Foliage of both species is usually very high above the ground, but the thick, corky, dark grayish-brown bark of Douglas-fir contrasts with the cinnamon-brown, vertically fissured bark of redwood.

Southernmost Coastal Douglas-Fir in United States

Finding the intriguing far-southern outlier of coastal Douglas-fir will be rewarding for the tree sleuth with a handheld GPS. In 1963 these trees were found inhabiting a sheltered gulch in the Purisima Hills about 5 miles northeast of Vandenberg Village and 10 miles from the ocean at 34°44′05″N, 120°25′05″W. This surprising grove was growing in Southern California 90 miles south of the species' previously recorded range limit in southern Monterey County, where Douglas-fir and redwood make their last stand as they encounter the increasingly arid coastal climate. This outlier stand was reported to cover 1 to 2 acres on an unusual white crumbly substrate called diatomaceous earth—nearly pure silica, which is the remains of fossilized algae that accumulated on a prehistoric seabed. (Diatomaceous earth has many uses in food, medicine, industry, and so forth.)

These Douglas-firs were thought to be a relict separated from the northern populations after the last ice age when the dry climate developed. Only sixteen mature Douglas-fir trees were found in 1963, the largest being 24 inches in diameter and 75 feet tall, but there were several hundred seedlings and saplings. The trees were enveloped in a dense stand of Bishop pine (*Pinus muricata*), a fire-adapted tree with closed cones that protect their enclosed seeds and release them into burned soil. Given the pine's relationship with fire, it is quite possible that since their 1963 discovery, the relict Douglas-firs may have burned in a severe wildfire, which adds to the mystery in seeking out this strange grove.

Yosemite

The enormously popular Yosemite Valley contains some of the Sierra Nevada's southernmost Douglas-firs. These coastal Douglas-fir trees reach great size. Two veterans growing near the roadhead at Mirror Lake, beneath the wall of Half Dome, are reported to be 7 feet in diameter and close to 200 feet tall, and John Muir described even larger ones. At Yosemite, Douglas-fir is largely confined to moist canyons, where visitors can find the big, corky-barked trees next to tumbling streams and waterfalls.

Colorado's Inland Douglas-Fir
Hermosa Creek: Outfitter Tree

It is a 4-mile hike up the Hermosa Creek Trail north of Durango, Colorado, to see the remains of the state's biggest Douglas-fir. Dubbed the Outfitter Tree because it was discovered by outfitter Sandy

Young, it has a 5.4-foot-diameter trunk and towers 163 feet tall. This Rocky Mountain giant, killed in a 2018 wildfire, stands along the popular trail above the confluence of Dutch Creek. Unusually large trees of other species also inhabit this drainage.

The Hermosa Creek trailhead is located at the end of Forest Road 576, accessed from US Highway 550 a few miles north of Durango. For maps, road, and trail conditions, visitors should consult the headquarters of the San Juan National Forest in Durango.

Idaho's Inland Douglas-Fir
Birch Creek Kilns

In the 1880s charcoal kilns were fueled by great quantities of Douglas-fir stripped off the high-desert mountains that parallel the sagebrush and grass landscape of the Birch Creek valley (see chapter 5). Reconstructed kilns and interpretive displays mark this National Historic Site, which is reached by a well-marked road on the west side of Idaho State Highway 28 a few miles north of its junction with Highway 22.

Craters of the Moon National Monument

A sharp-eyed visitor can spot straight Douglas-firs projecting from small, sheltered depressions amid the black lava flows sparsely covered with sprawling limber pines and bushy junipers. One such example is visible along an early part of the park's loop drive.

Monida Pass

High-elevation, pure Douglas-fir stands adjoin the west side of Interstate 15 about halfway between Monida Pass on the Continental Divide and the village of Spencer, Idaho. There is a wide pull-off spot on the west side amid these trees.

Montana's Inland Douglas-Fir
Glacier Park Lodge

Although only the inland variety of Douglas-fir is native to Montana, the historic Glacier Park Lodge features massive nonnative coastal Douglas-fir timbers. The hotel is located on the east side of Glacier National Park, at the gateway to stunning alpine scenery.

Groundwork for the magnificent hotel began when Louis Hill, son of railroad magnate James J. Hill, stepped down from his position as president of the Great Northern Railway in 1910 to focus his energies on constructing a destination hotel in the Montana Rockies. The politically well-connected Hill took the first step of what seemed an impossible dream by lobbying Congress to obtain national park status for Glacier. His efforts paid off, as Congress designated Glacier a national park in 1910. A follow-up act of Congress in 1912 granted him negotiating rights to buy a 160-acre parcel within the Blackfeet Indian Reservation located just opposite the Great Northern railroad depot in East Glacier. Hotel construction began immediately. An earlier visit to the Forestry Building at the 1905 Lewis and Clark Centennial Exposition in Portland, Oregon, deeply impressed Hill, who used the layout of that building's Grand Hall as the centerpiece of his Glacier Park Hotel design.

Soaring, 40-foot-tall Douglas-fir timbers, with diameters ranging from 36 to 42 inches, were erected to form a massive colonnade delineating the spacious hotel lobby. Carefully selected coastal Douglas-fir trees were cut in early spring before the sap had risen to ensure that the bark stayed intact. The timbers were then shipped by rail from Oregon to East Glacier, where workmen faced the monumental task of transporting the huge pieces from the railroad cars to the building site without damaging the bark.

Fifteen months after construction started, Glacier Park Lodge opened for business. Hill advertised Glacier Park as the "American Alps," and the 61-room hotel was overbooked as soon as it opened. The immense timbers prompted the Blackfeet Indians to call it

Omahkoyis, meaning "Big Tree Lodge," which soon became the hotel's well-deserved nickname. Over the next dozen years, Hill and the Great Northern Railway would build several more Swiss-chalet-style hotels in Glacier, as well as the British-themed Prince of Wales Hotel in adjacent Waterton Lakes National Park. Despite the stiff competition, Glacier Park Lodge and its visually stunning Douglas-fir columns retained the top spot in the park's hotel pecking order. An updated and enlarged version of the hotel still beckons visitors from around the world over a century later.

Glacier Park Lodge is located on the left side of Montana Highway 49 in East Glacier Park, about a tenth of a mile west of the junction with US Highway 2.

 ### Lewis and Clark Pass: Shrubby Douglas-Fir

This 6200-foot pass is a spectacular "wind funnel" atop the Continental Divide, where a host of dwarf woodland, alpine tundra, and mountain grassland plants form a mosaic representing different microenvironments. The frequent hurricane-force winds experienced here, especially as part of snow- and ice-blasting blizzards in winter, give rise to this strange dwarf woodland. This type of vegetation usually occurs only well above 8000 feet. The trees, including Douglas-fir, lodgepole pine, limber pine, aspen, and others, are so frequently battered with gales and strong winds that they take the form of bushy or tall, gangly shrubs.

For hundreds and probably thousands of years, Indian tribes used this mountain saddle to travel over the backbone of the Rockies. Explorers Lewis and Clark learned about the route from Indians they encountered. Lewis led part of the Corps of Discovery eastward over this pass in 1806, while Clark led the remainder of their party on a southern route across what is now Montana.

Lewis and Clark Pass is reached by a relatively easy 2-mile hike from the trailhead at the end of Alice Creek Road, which heads north off Montana Highway 200 east of Lincoln.

South Fork Teton River: Rare Douglas-Fir of Montana's Rocky Mountain Front

Most trails heading west into the Front Range of the Rockies lead through steep, rocky canyons and areas where wind-driven wildfires have prevented development of mature Douglas-firs. An exception lies at the end of the long, narrow canyon carved deep into the Front Range by the South Fork Teton River, west of Choteau, Montana. Here a 3.5-mile-long trail heads up to the subalpine gem called Our Lake. The trail climbs through well-developed forest and undergrowth communities unusual for the Rocky Mountain Front. Mature subalpine fir, spruce, and lodgepole pine are accompanied by some impressive old inland Douglas-firs at least 2.5 feet wide and about 100 feet tall.

Rocky Mountain Front: Wind-Sculpted Douglas-Fir

A seemingly endless wall of snow-clad mountains rising abruptly from the vast Great Plains in north-central Montana is visible from 100 miles out on the plains. This massive escarpment captivated Lewis and Clark and other early Euro-American adventurers. Stretching from southwest of Augusta, Montana, to the southern boundary of Alberta, and including the east side of Glacier National Park, the incomparable panorama continues to entrance people.

The Rocky Mountain Front is a land of beauty, amazing plant diversity, and an extremely harsh climate. The Front, as locals call it, is frequented by mighty winds sweeping south through Alberta that usher in Arctic air masses. Then Chinook winds, which are warm westerly air masses, roar in across the Continental Divide and abruptly raise winter temperatures 60° Fahrenheit or more. Even in spring and summer, visitors are advised to keep track of wind forecasts.

The harsh climate together with excessively well-drained limestone soils produces unique plant communities. For example, ponderosa pine, so widespread in Montana and other western states, disappears in the Rocky Mountain Front. Instead, an extensive dwarf woodland of Douglas-fir, limber pine, and juniper spreads out onto the western edge of the high plains.

A good place to see this unusual belt of thick-canopied, wind-trained Douglas-fir is on the road to the Blackleaf Canyon trailhead northwest of Choteau; but beware of entering the slot gorge just past the trailhead if a gale is blowing. The gorge is a notorious wind-tunnel where a hurricane-force blast can knock hikers off their feet. In spring, visitors to the pygmy forest on the plains east of the trailhead are rewarded with a rich community of brightly colored wildflowers, some of which are indigenous to the limestone soils.

Bitterroot National Forest: Douglas-Fir Grassland and Historical Indian Trees

One forest road branching off from US Highway 93 at the south end of the Bitterroot Valley reveals two contrasting features of Douglas-fir forest. The short, well-maintained part of the road leads to Indian Trees Campground, which contains ancient living artifacts of American Indian subsistence in the form of bark-peeled old-growth ponderosa pines. These are being invaded and crowded out by young Douglas-firs as a result of the elimination of fire. The other road branch climbs about 3000 feet in elevation, partially on a long, single-lane route, to a rare landscape of Douglas-fir grassland and spectacular panoramas above the limit of ponderosa pine.

To visit these unique places, take Forest Road 13340 signed for Indian Trees Campground, which branches off the west side of Highway 93 immediately before it starts a steep climb from the Sula Valley heading toward Lost Trail Pass on the Montana-Idaho state line. After about three-quarters of a mile, take the right-hand branch road to Indian Trees. Even before entering the campground, some of the big ancient bark-peeled ponderosas and young invading Douglas-firs are visible. A display at the entrance shows how Indian women peeled the sap-rich inner bark of these pines in spring to sweeten and preserve dried fruit and nut mixtures (pemmican) and to prolong the life of the cord they made from deer and elk tendons or sinew. The upper Bitterroot River drainages have the highest known concentration of these Indian bark-peeled trees. Professor Lars Östlund and his students from Umeå University in Sweden documented 274 Indian trees in only two areas they studied in these drainages.

Adventurous visitors can experience the Douglas-fir–grassland landscape by returning a short distance toward the highway and turning right onto Forest Road 8112 signed for Porcupine Saddle. Check in advance with the main office for the Bitterroot National Forest in Hamilton about current road conditions, but it is usually open by mid-June, and is popular with locals. A high-clearance vehicle is necessary because stones sometimes roll onto the narrow sidehill stretch as it climbs to 7000-foot Porcupine Saddle. Once at the flat saddle, a three-quarter-mile trail starting on the north end of the parking area leads west to join Warm Springs Ridge Trail (Trail 178). Head north (right) at that junction for a half mile to reach a rounded 7600-foot rock outcrop with a panorama of Douglas-fir grassland in the foreground and wild high country extending to distant horizons.

Nevada's Douglas-Fir
Cave Rock: Solitary Coastal Douglas-Fir

Douglas-fir's appearance in Nevada is highly concentrated. The inland variety is restricted to just a few mountain ranges in east-central Nevada, where it is typically found on cool, moist north and east slopes. In stark contrast, an impressive coastal Douglas-fir tree appears in extreme west-central Nevada on the sun-drenched east shore of Lake Tahoe. The tree grows about a mile north of Cave Rock, a geological attraction and state park. Finding the tree requires persistence; it grows in a depression about midway between US Highway 50 and the lakeshore, in mixture with Jeffrey pine and incense cedar, and despite its nearly 140-foot height and 5-foot diameter, the tree can easily be overlooked.

What makes this tree unique is that it is the only known occurrence of coastal Douglas-fir in the state of Nevada, and the only naturally occurring coastal Douglas-fir found outside the three Pacific coastal states or the province of British Columbia. Professor David Charlet, an authority on Nevada's natural vegetation, says it is the only specimen of this variety of Douglas-fir that he's found in over thirty years of studying the state's flora and mountain ranges. It seems likely that a few other individual trees or clumps of coastal Douglas-fir exist in the Lake Tahoe area of Nevada or in forested areas farther north, but they remain undiscovered if they do.

Interested visitors can park at the Logan Shoals Vista Point on the west side of Highway 50 and pick their way a short quarter of a mile south and southwest from the parking area to the vicinity of the tree.

 Highest-Elevation Inland Douglas-Fir

Despite Nevada's very minor representation of Douglas-fir, it features a couple of especially notable individual trees: the only coastal Douglas-fir tree growing in a state not bordering the Pacific Ocean (see preceding entry), and a record-breaking specimen of inland Douglas-fir growing near the state's eastern edge, both found by Professor David Charlet. Inland Douglas-fir is occasionally found on cool, moist north and east slopes in the eastern mountains of the state, including the Snake Range, the White Rock Mountains, and the Wilson Peak Range. Prior to Charlet's findings, the highest-elevation occurrence for an individual inland Douglas-fir was 10,706 feet on Mount Graham in southeast Arizona. However, Charlet found an inland Douglas-fir growing at 10,968 feet in the Snake Range, a full 262 feet higher than the previous record. What makes this specimen unique is that Charlet found it growing on the warm, sunny southwest slope of Mount Washington less than 700 feet from the summit, instead of on a cooler, moister north or east slope.

A surprising diversity of trees can be found in Nevada's desert mountain ranges, including some bristlecone pines. An extensive stand of ancient and photogenic Great Basin bristlecone pines lies just northeast of Mount Washington in the Snake Range. It is located in seldom-visited Great Basin National Park, just west of the Nevada-Utah border and the tiny town of Baker, Nevada. Wheeler Peak, the second-highest peak in Nevada at 13,065 feet, is also located in the park. Inquire with park staff for directions and the best hiking route to the Mount Washington summit area (elevation 11,658 feet).

New Mexico's Inland Douglas-Fir
El Malpais National Monument: Yoda

Some trees become icons because of awe-inspiring physical dimensions, such as California's General Sherman sequoia (275 feet high, 25 feet wide), others because they played a key role in history, such as British Columbia's Lillooet Hanging Tree (used as a gallows during the Fraser River gold rush). Less clear is how a tiny, misshapen Douglas-fir growing on a barren lava bed at the El Malpais National Monument in New Mexico achieved national acclaim.

The gnarly 7-foot-tall Douglas-fir, affectionately named Yoda after the *Star Wars* character, had undeniable visual appeal. Henri Grissino-Mayer, a noted tree-ring scientist, first saw Yoda in the early 1990s. He aged the tree at 650 years, making it the oldest known Douglas-fir in New Mexico at the time. The tree was in good health: a 1993 photo shows it had a short, thick crown loaded with cones. But by 2010, Yoda's crown was noticeably thinning. Grant Harley, a professor from Mississippi, reported that Yoda was alive in the spring of 2014; however, by the time he returned with a group of graduate students that August, the tree had died. Even before then, Yoda had gained national attention.

Despite its diminutive stature, this tree had far-reaching scientific importance. Yoda, and a smattering of other ancient conifers growing on droughty sites scattered across the Southwest, provided scientists an invaluable source of data. The widths of the annual growth rings on these venerable trees reflect usable moisture from one year to the next, far back into the past. Developing relationships between tree-ring widths and climate during periods for which weather records are available allows scientists to estimate precipitation in the past and predict future climatic scenarios. (See also chapter 1.)

In September 2014, reporter John Fleck wrote the equivalent of an obituary for Yoda in the *Albuquerque Journal*. Similar stories appeared in *Earth Notes, NBC News*, the *Taos News*, the *Wall Street Journal*, and other major outlets, ensuring that this tree's unique appeal and scientific contribution would be recorded in perpetuity.

Yoda's dead bole still stands. For its exact location, check with rangers at either of the two visitor centers, one at El Malpais National Monument and the other in Grants, New Mexico.

 ### Oregon's Coastal Douglas-Fir
Barlow Road: Snub Trees

The Oregon Trail—sometimes referred to as the nation's longest graveyard—was replete with perils that caused the death of nearly one in ten people along the way. The final stretch required emigrants to negotiate the treacherous waters of the Lower Columbia River by raft before arriving at Oregon City and the Willamette Valley. However, beginning in 1846, emigrants were provided an alternative to the dreaded river route.

The Barlow Road, which blazed the route known today as US Highway 26, or Mount Hood Scenic Highway, was chopped through the dense Douglas-fir forests along the south and southwest flanks of the mountain. One obstacle along the Barlow Road, known as the Laurel Hill Chute, was located about halfway between the present-day communities of Government Camp and Rhododendron. The precipitous 300-foot incline at first seemed impassable, but at this stage of the journey the hardened travelers were not about to turn back. Rawhide ropes were wrapped around Douglas-fir "snub" trees at the top of the hill, which served as a drag or brake as the emigrants slowly lowered their covered wagons down the chute to the gently sloping road below. Some of the rope-burned Douglas-firs atop Laurel Hill are still standing today, well over a century and a half later.

How important was the Barlow Road? Matthew Deady, Oregon's first federal judge, asserted that "the construction of the Barlow Road contributed more towards the prosperity of the Willamette Valley and the future State of Oregon, than any other achievement prior to the building of the railways in 1870."

H. J. Andrews Experimental Forest

Visitors are invited to see, hike through, and learn about the impressive old-growth coastal Douglas-fir at this experimental forest maintained by Oregon State University. The area is reached via Oregon Route 126 heading east up the McKenzie River from Eugene.

Lake Oswego's Peg Tree

In 2010 the city of Lake Oswego, Oregon (south of Portland) initiated the Century Tree Project, seeking out trees at least one hundred years old that had a link to the past. A half century earlier, author Mary Goodall colorfully described the historical significance of Douglas-fir trees to the area: "The Indian trail to Oswego lay like a frayed brown ribbon gently placed between the masses of giant fir trees above the Willamette River. . . . These trees were essential to Native lifeways: they made canoes from Douglas-firs and wove fishing nets from its roots."

One notable specimen selected for the Century Tree Project was the Peg Tree, a stout, thick-barked Douglas-fir located at 141 Leonard Street in the Old Town district of Lake Oswego. Records show that the tree served as the growing community's general gathering place. A lantern was hung from a peg in the tree to light evening town meetings, hence the name. Starting in 1852, the city's first Sunday school classes were also held under the tree for lack of a church or other suitable building. Not all agree whether vestiges of the peg hole are still visible in the tree, but the peg can be viewed at the nearby Oswego Heritage House and Museum, where it is stored for safekeeping.

Oregon's Inland Douglas-Fir
Wallowa Mountains: Old-Growth Inland Douglas-Fir

Ecologist Charles Johnson's detailed publication on high mountain vegetation, *Alpine and Subalpine Vegetation of the Wallowa, Seven Devils, and Blue Mountains*, describes and depicts stands of old-growth inland Douglas-fir. Many of these stands grow in remote areas, but one is easily found alongside a US Forest Service road that provides access to a trail leading into the high country of the impressive Wallowa Mountains. The Tenderfoot Road (Forest Road 100) provides access to the trailhead at 6500 feet. A pure Douglas-fir forest inhabits the dry, rocky south-facing slopes. Craggy-barked trees adorned with yellow and chartreuse staghorn lichens are up to 3 feet in diameter and mostly two hundred to three hundred years old. They exhibit black scars from surface fires that burned in times past.

To reach the Tenderfoot trailhead, travel east on Oregon Route 350 from the town of Joseph for 8 miles and then turn right (south) on Oregon Route 39, also known as the Hells Canyon Scenic Byway. Follow this road, which eventually becomes FR 39, for 13 miles past Salt Creek Summit, and then turn right on FR 100, which reaches the old-growth Douglas-firs and the Tenderfoot trailhead shortly.

Texas's Inland Douglas-Fir
Guadalupe and Chisos Mountains: Elusive Douglas-Fir

Douglas-fir occurs at upper elevations of the Guadalupe Mountains in Guadalupe National Park in far west Texas just south of the New Mexico border, but the trees are several thousand feet above and several miles beyond the nearest trailhead. There are also uncon-firmed reports of Douglas-fir atop the Chisos Mountains in Big Bend National Park. The head of Boot Canyon above 7000 feet would be a likely location as it shelters Arizona cypress (*Cupressus arizo-nica*) and a number of high-elevation moist-site species. Also, the Boot Canyon Trail, which begins at 5400-foot Chisos Basin, offers some amazing views, including colorful mountain walls dropping down thousands of feet into the vast wildlands of northern Mexico. Another reward is seeing the canyon's namesake "boot," a spectac-ular 200-foot-tall pinnacle that resembles an upside-down leg with a cowboy boot atop it. Anyone who finds Douglas-firs or reasonable facsimiles here should record the exact location and take photos of the trees, including close-ups of foliage, and make them available to park naturalists. Such a find would be notable because the Chisos Mountains are more than 100 miles south of any confirmed Doug-las-fir occurrence in the United States.

 Utah's Inland Douglas-Fir
Bryce Canyon National Park: Douglas-Firs of Wall Street

Southern Utah is a geological wonderland, eroded over millennia into a labyrinth of canyons and red-, orange-, and pink-hued col-umns, or hoodoos. The Navajo Loop Trail in Bryce Canyon, a pop-ular hiking route heading southeast from Sunset Point, provides visitors unparalleled views of hoodoos and slot canyons from top to bottom. The trail descends sharply through a series of switchbacks to a section called Wall Street, so named because canyon walls tower like skyscrapers over passing hikers. Here, squeezed between sheer rock walls, a half-dozen or so centuries-old Douglas-firs jut skyward from the barren canyon floor. But these are not just average trees. They are magnificent, clean-boled trees reaching for the small strip of sky far overhead.

The Navajo Loop Trail is the most popular trail in Bryce, and the Wall Street section—graced by remarkable Douglas-firs growing in such an unexpected place—is the overwhelming favorite part of the loop for hikers. A trail map can be downloaded from the Bryce Canyon National Park website. The Wall Street section of the Navajo Loop is closed seasonally and when rain is imminent, so visitors are advised to call ahead at Bryce Canyon for up-to-date trail information.

Washington's Coastal Douglas-Fir
Grove of the Patriarchs

A visit to the most famous giant coastal Douglas-firs on Mount Rainier is especially memorable because of its unique access. The trail to the Grove of the Patriarchs features ancient Douglas-firs, western redcedars, and hemlocks growing on an island in the glacier-fed Ohanapecosh River, accessed by a swaying suspension bridge. The trailhead to the island grove is located along the Stevens Canyon Road about a quarter mile past the park's entrance station on Washington State Route 123, 14 miles east of Packwood. When the road crosses the bridge over the Ohanapecosh River, the trailhead parking area appears on the right. The suspension bridge lies about a half mile up the trail and should be crossed by only one person at a time.

 Hurricane Ridge

Located atop a 5200-foot prominence, Hurricane Ridge provides spectacular views into the heart of the Olympic Mountains. It also affords easy access to scattered Douglas-firs growing with patches of subalpine firs mixed with high mountain meadows not far below the timberline. A few very old hunched-over Douglas-firs still survive on the wind-blasted slope rising northeast from the visitor center toward a 5450-foot ridge point. These stout, bent-over trees have thick, almost ground-hugging canopies that provide shelter for blacktail does and their fawns when summer storms burst onto the idyllic high-country meadows. Hurricane Ridge in Olympic National Park is about 20 miles south of Port Angeles.

Rockport State Park

This state park is a little-known enclave of giant old coastal Douglas-firs in the heavily logged valley of the Skagit River. The park's 670 acres of valley-bottom forest boast 5 miles of hiking trails. It is located adjacent to the tiny town of Rockport along the North Cascades Highway, 35 miles east of Interstate 5.

 Staircase Area of Olympic National Park

In the southeast corner of Olympic National Park, Staircase offers easy access to rain forests where Douglas-firs 5 to 9 feet thick and more than 200 feet tall dwarf old bigleaf maples draped with hanging clubmoss. Near the Skokomish River, somewhat smaller but equally tall grand firs accompany the towering Douglas-firs. The trail leading up the river from Staircase threads a passage through these magnificent trees, and a short way up it passes through vestiges of a severe 1985 wildfire. Covered with heavily charred bark, some of the old-growth Douglas-firs that survived this fire are now engulfed in a sea of young Douglas-firs that are outgrowing the accompanying hemlocks.

 Washington's Inland Douglas-Fir
North-Central and Northeastern Washington Hiking Trails

Some of the high-elevation forest roads and trails up south-facing slopes and ridges of the Okanogan Range northeast of Winthrop on the Okanogan National Forest access old inland Douglas-firs mixed with grassland. This road and trail system leads to the highest peak, 8242-foot Tiffany Mountain. Farther east the Kettle Crest Trail is reached from 5577-foot Sherman Pass on Washington State Route 20 east of Republic. With mountains reaching as high as 7000 feet, the Kettle Range is not as dry as the Okanogan Range, but old Douglas-firs are likely still to be seen on the west-facing side of the crest trail. At lower elevations, especially in the drier forests above the valley bottoms east of Republic, Douglas-fir is commonly seen replacing the historically dominant ponderosa pine and western larch.

 Wyoming's Inland Douglas-Fir
Yellowstone National Park's Historical Douglas-Fir Forests

Remnants of the historical Douglas-fir forest and savanna are found at Mammoth Hot Springs in Yellowstone National Park and along stretches of the park's 45-mile drive heading east to just past Soda Butte. Some of these forests and savannas burned in the huge 1988 wildfires, and in moist areas big old Douglas-firs were killed, their snags and downed trunks still visible but now engulfed in a profusion of young lodgepole pines. Prior to 1900 these forests burned often enough so that big Douglas-firs survived. Some relict Douglas-fir stands can be seen around Tower Junction.

The historic Roosevelt Lodge, built there to commemorate a camping trip by President Theodore Roosevelt, is composed of Douglas-fir logs with the bark still attached. These are likely from coastal Douglas-firs shipped in a century ago because of the limbiness and excessive taper of the nearby and then-abundant big inland Douglas-firs. An additional irony here is that President Chester Arthur camped at the site in 1883, but President Teddy Roosevelt never did!

REFERENCES

The following books, articles, journals, and websites provided background and informed our research. While we have taken precautions to ensure that the content of this book is accurate and up-to-date, it is impossible to include all sources because of the very broad scope of subjects presented and the fact that we consulted a variety of online sources.

INTRODUCTION

Arno, S. F., J. H. Scott, and M. G. Hartwell. "Age-Class Structure of Old Growth Ponderosa Pine/Douglas-Fir Stands and Its Relation to Fire History." US Forest Service Intermountain Research Station, Research Paper INT-RP-481, 1995.

Arno, S. F., H. Y. Smith, and M. A. Krebs. "Old Growth Ponderosa Pine and Western Larch Stand Structures: Influences of Pre-1900 Fires and Fire Exclusion." US Forest Service Intermountain Research Station, Research Paper INT-RP-495, 1997.

Pfister, R. D., B. Kovalchik, S. Arno, and R. Presby. "Forest Habitat Types of Montana." US Forest Service Intermountain Research Station, General Technical Report INT-GTP-34, 1977.

Steele, R., R. D. Pfister, R. A. Ryker, and J. A. Kittams. "Forest Habitat Types of Central Idaho." US Forest Service Intermountain Research Station, General Technical Report INT-114, 1981.

CHAPTER 1

"*Abies Douglasii.*" *Penny Cyclopaedia* 1 (1833): 32. London: Society for the Diffusion of Useful Knowledge.

Adams, R. P., J. J. Vargas-Hernández, M. S. González Elizondo, G. Hunter, T. A. Fairhall, D. Thornburg, and F. Callahan. "Taxonomy of Douglas Fir (*Pseudotsuga menziesii*) Infraspecific Taxa: vars. *menziesii, glauca* and *oaxacana*: nrDNA, cpDNA Sequences and Leaf Essential Oils." *Phytologia* 95 (2013): 94–102.

Beiler K. J., D. M. Durall, S. W. Simard, S. A. Maxwell, and A. M. Kretzer. "Architecture of the Wood-Wide Web: *Rhizopogon* spp. Genets Link Multiple Douglas-Fir Cohorts." *New Phytologist* 185, no. 2 (2009): 543–553.

Bilby R. E., E. W. Beach, B. R. Fransen, J. K. Walter, and P. A. Bisson. "Transfer of Nutrients from Spawning Salmon to Riparian Vegetation in Western Washington." *Transactions of the American Fisheries Society* 132, no. 4 (2003): 733–745.

Brubaker, L. B. "Climate Change and the Origin of Old-Growth Douglas-Fir Forests in the Puget Sound Lowland." US Forest Service Pacific Northwest Research Station, General Technical Report PNW-GTR-285, 1991: 17–32. www.fs.fed.us /pnw/pubs/gtr285/gtr2852a.pdf.

Burns, J. N., R. Acuna-Soto, and D. W. Stahle. "Drought and Epidemic Typhus, Central Mexico, 1655–1918." *Emerging Infectious Diseases* 20, no. 3 (2014): 442–447. www.ncbi.nlm.nih.gov/pmc/articles/PMC3944858.

Carder, A. C. *Forest Giants of the World: Past and Present.* Markham, ON: Fitzhenry and Whiteside, 1995.

Cole, J. E. "The Cone-Bearing Trees of Yosemite." *Yosemite Nature Notes* 18 (1939): 33–72.

Coupar, D. "Which Is the Biggest of Them All?" *MacMillan Bloedel News,* November 1970, 6.

Debreczy, Z., and I. Rácz. "New Species and Varieties of Conifers from Mexico." *Phytologia* 78, no. 4 (1995): 217–243.

Frothingham, E. H. "Douglas-Fir (*Pseudotsuga taxifolia* [Lam.] Britton): A Study of the Rocky Mountain and Pacific Coast Forms." US Department of Agriculture Forest Service Circular 150, 1909.

Gorzelak M., A. K. Asay, B. J. Pickles, and S. W. Simard. "Inter-plant Communication through Mycorrhizal Networks Mediates Complex Adaptive Behaviour in Plant Communities." *AoB Plants* 7 (2015): plv050.

Green, M. L. "Rules of Botanical Nomenclature." *Empire Forestry Journal* 10, no. 1 (1931): 54–72.

Grissino-Mayer, H. D. "A 2129-Year Reconstruction of Precipitation for Northwestern New Mexico, USA." In *Tree Rings, Environment, and Humanity,* ed. J. S. Dean, D. M. Meko, and T. W. Swetnam, 191–204. Tucson: *Radiocarbon,* Department of Geosciences, University of Arizona, 1996.

———. "Tree-Ring Reconstructions of Climate and Fire History at El Malpais National Monument, New Mexico." PhD dissertation, University of Arizona, 1995.

Gugger, P. F, A. González-Rodríguez, H. Rodríguez-Correa, S. Sugita, and J. Cavender-Bares. "Southward Pleistocene Migration of Douglas-Fir into Mexico: Phylogeography, Ecological Niche Modeling, and Conservation of 'Rear Edge' Populations." *New Phytologist* 189, no 4. (2011): 1185–1199.

Harr, R. Dennis. "Fog Drip in the Bull Run Municipal Watershed, Oregon." *Journal of the American Water Resources Association* 18, no. 5 (1982): 785–789.

Hermann, D. K. *The Genus Pseudotsuga: Historical Records and Nomenclature.* Forest Research Laboratory Special Publication 2a, Oregon State University, Corvallis, 1982.

Howe, G. T. "Bibliography of Douglas-Fir Ecological Genetics, Evolutionary Genetics, Physiological Genetics, and Tree Breeding." Pacific Northwest Research Cooperative Report 24, Oregon State University, Corvallis, 2006.

"Key Events in the Life of David Douglas." Oregon Cultural Heritage Commission, 2014. Accessed Nov. 3, 2019. www.findingdaviddouglas.org/timeline.php.

Kinver, Mark. "Water's the Limit for Tall Trees." *BBC News,* August 13, 2008. Accessed Nov. 3, 2019. http://news.bbc.co.uk/2/hi/science/nature/7556065.stm.

Krajina, V. J. "A Summary of the Nomenclature of Douglas-Fir." *Madroño* 13 (1956): 265–267.

Lanner, R. M. "Living Stumps in the Sierra Nevada." *Ecology* 42, no. 1 (1961): 170–173.

Lavender, D. P., and R. K. Hermann. *Douglas-Fir: The Genus Pseudotsuga*. Forest Research Laboratory, Oregon State University, Corvallis, 2014.

Little, Elbert L., Jr. "The Genus *Pseudotsuga* (Douglas-Fir) in North America." *Leaflets of Western Botany* 6 (1952): 181–198.

Maiden, J. H. "The International Rules of Botanical Nomenclature (Adopted by the International Botanical Congress, Vienna, 1905)." *Journal and Proceedings of the Royal Society of New South Wales* 40 (1906): 74–94.

Marks, J. A., J. C. Pett-Ridge, S. S. Perakis, J. L. Allen, and B. McCune. "Response of the Nitrogen-Fixing Lichen *Lobaria pulmonaria* to Phosphorus, Molybdenum, and Vanadium." *Ecosphere* 6, no. 9 (2015): 1–17.

Martínez, M. "Las *Pseudotsugas* de México." *Anales del Instituto de Biología* 20 (1949): 129–184.

Neale, D. B., and K. V. Krutovsky. "Comparative Genetic Mapping in Trees: The Group of Conifers." In *Molecular Marker Systems in Plant Breeding and Crop Improvement*, ed. H. Lörz and G. Wenzel, 267–277. *Biotechnology in Agriculture and Forestry* 55. Berlin: Springer, 2007.

Nisbet, J. *The Collector: David Douglas and the Natural History of the Northwest*. Seattle: Sasquatch Books, 2009.

Reveal, James L. "Douglas-Fir: A Nomenclatural Morass." *Discovering Lewis & Clark*. Accessed Nov. 6, 2019. www.lewis-clark.org/article/1509.

Sillett, S. C. "Branch Epiphyte Assemblages in the Forest Interior and on the Clearcut Edge of a 700-Year-Old Douglas Fir Canopy in Western Oregon." *The Bryologist* 98, no. 3 (1995): 301–312.

Sudworth, George Bishop. *Forest Trees of the Pacific Slope*. US Department of Agriculture, Forest Service. Washington, DC: Government Printing Office, 1908.

Suzuki, David, and Wayne Grady. *Tree: A Life Story*. Vancouver, BC: Greystone Books, 2004.

Teste, F. P., S. W. Simard, D. M. Durall, R. D. Guy, M. D. Jones, and A. L. Schoonmaker. "Access to Mycorrhizal Networks and Roots of Trees: Importance for Seedling Survival and Resource Transfer." *Ecology* 90, no. 10 (2009): 2808–2822.

University of Toronto/Université Laval and M. L. Tyrwhitt-Drake. "Douglas, David." In *Dictionary of Canadian Biography*, vol. 6. University of Toronto/Université Laval, 2003. Accessed Nov. 6, 2019. www.biographi.ca/en/bio/douglas_david_6E.html.

Van Pelt, Robert. *Forest Giants of the Pacific Coast*. Seattle: University of Washington Press, 2001.

Vancouver Island Big Trees (blog). "Douglas-Fir Stumps Healed by Helpful Neighbours." April 13, 2013. Accessed Nov. 3, 2019. https://vancouverislandbigtrees.blogspot.com/2013/04/douglas-fir-stumps-healed-by-helpful.html.

Waring, R. H., and J. F. Franklin. "Evergreen Coniferous Forests of the Pacific Northwest." *Science* 204 (1979): 1380–1386.

CHAPTER 2

Little, Elbert L., Jr. Vol. 1 of *Atlas of United States Trees*. US Department of Agriculture Miscellaneous Publication 1146. Map 80. 1971.

Muir, John. "The Forests of Oregon and Their Inhabitants." In *Wilderness Essays*. Layton, UT: Gibbs Smith, 1918.

Pinchot, Gifford. *Breaking New Ground*. New York: Harcourt, Brace, 1947.

Van Pelt, Robert. *Forest Giants of the Pacific Coast*. Seattle: University of Washington Press, 2001.

Western Lumberman. "Coast and Mountain News." January 1910, 16.

CHAPTER 3

BC Parks. "Takla Lake." British Columbia Ministry of Environment, Ecological Reserve 38, 2019. Accessed Oct. 30, 2019. www.env.gov.bc.ca/bcparks /eco_reserve/takla_er/Takla%20Lake%20ER%2038.pdf?v=1471820690907.

Cruickshank, A. "Setting Fires to Prevent Fires: Prescribed Burns Planned This Spring Near Cariboo-Chilcotin and Kamloops, B.C. to Help Restore Grasslands." thestar.com, April 25, 2018. www.thestar.com/vancouver/2018/04/25 /prescribed-burns-used-to-restore-traditional-grasslands.html.

Earle, C., ed. "*Pseudotsuga menziesii* subsp. *glauca*." The Gymnosperm Database. Accessed Oct. 30, 2019. www.conifers.org/pi/Pseudotsuga_menziesii_glauca .php.

Eckenwalder, James E. *Conifers of the World: The Complete Reference*. Portland, OR: Timber Press, 2009.

Fiedler, Carl E., and Stephen F. Arno. *Ponderosa: People, Fire, and the West's Most Iconic Tree*. Missoula, MT: Mountain Press, 2015.

Gruell, G. E. "Fire and Vegetative Trends in the Northern Rockies." US Forest Service Intermountain Research Station, General Technical Report INT-GTR-158, 1983.

Gugger, P. F., A. González-Rodríguez, H. Rodríguez-Correa, S. Sugita, and J. Cavender-Bares. "Southward Pleistocene Migration of Douglas-Fir into Mexico: Phylogeography, Ecological Niche Modeling, and Conservation of 'Rear Edge' Populations." *New Phytologist* 189, no. 4 (2011): 1185–1199.

Hamann, A., and T. Wang. "Potential Effects of Climate Change on Ecosystem and Tree Species Distribution in British Columbia." *Ecology* 87, no. 11 (2006): 2773–2786.

Lanner, Ronald M. *Trees of the Great Basin: A Natural History*. Reno: University of Nevada Press, 1984.

Little, Elbert L., Jr. Vol. 1 of *Atlas of United States Trees*. US Department of Agriculture Miscellaneous Publication 1146. Map 80. 1971.

McLean, Alastair. "History of the Cattle Industry in British Columbia." *Rangelands* 4, no. 3 (June 1982): 130–134. www.cattlemen.bc.ca/docs/history.pdf.

Monserud, R. A., and G. E. Rehfeldt. "Genetic and Environmental Components of Variation of Site Index in Inland Douglas-Fir." *Forest Science* 36, no. 1 (1990): 1–9.

Pfister, R. D., B. Kovalchik, S. Arno, and R. Presby. "Forest Habitat Types of Montana." US Forest Service Intermountain Research Station, General Technical Report INT-GTR-34, 1977.

Rehfeldt, G. E. "Ecological Adaptations in Douglas-Fir (*Pseudotsuga menziesii* var. *glauca*): A Synthesis." *Forest Ecology and Management* 28, nos. 3–4 (1989): 203–215.

Rodebaugh, Dale. "State Champion: Douglas Fir North of Town Is Colo.'s Tallest." *Durango Herald*, July 25, 2014.

Steele, B., and C. Fiedler. "Kalman Filter Analysis of Growth–Climate Relations in Old-Growth Ponderosa Pine and Douglas-Fir Stands." *Radiocarbon* 38 (1996): 303–314.

Strauss, S. H., A. H. Doerksen, and J. R. Byrne. "Evolutionary Relationships of Doug-las-Fir and Its Relatives (Genus *Pseudotsuga*) from DNA Restriction Fragment Analysis." *Canadian Journal of Botany* 68, no. 7 (1990): 1502–1510.

Swanson, Frederick Harold. *The Bitterroot and Mr. Brandborg: Clearcutting and the Struggle for Sustainable Forestry in the Northern Rockies.* Salt Lake City: University of Utah Press, 2011.

"2015 Montana Register of Big Trees." Montana Department of Natural Resources and Conservation. Accessed Oct. 30, 2019. http://dnrc.mt.gov/divisions /forestry/docs/assistance/big-tree/2014_bigtreeregister.pdf.

CHAPTER 4

Bryan, Dan. "Early Washington and the Logging and Timber Industry." American History USA, 2012. Accessed Nov. 6, 2019. www.americanhistoryusa.com /early-washington-and-logging-timber-industry.

Center for the Study of the Pacific Northwest. "The Rise of the Lumber Industry, 1848–1883." University of Washington, Seattle. Accessed Nov. 6, 2019. www .washington.edu/uwired/outreach/cspn/Website/Classroom%20Materials /Curriculum%20Packets/Evergreen%20State/Section%20II.html.

Clark, Brian Charles. "Wood Takes Wing." *Washington State Magazine*, Winter 2016: 25.

Coman, Edwin T., Jr., and Helen M. Gibbs. *Time, Tide and Timber: A Century of Pope and Talbot.* Palo Alto, CA: Stanford University Press, 1949.

Dietrich, William. "Douglas Fir, Then and Now." *Seattle Times*, March 19, 2000.

Gibbs, James A. *Shipwrecks of the Pacific Coast.* Portland, OR: Binfords and Mort, 1957.

Gordon, Greg. *When Money Grew on Trees: A. B. Hammond and the Age of the Timber Baron.* Norman: University of Oklahoma Press, 2014.

Grant, Richard. "John Steinbeck's Epic Ocean Voyage Rewrote the Rules of Ecology." *Smithsonian*, September 2019.

Johnson, Larry E. "Puget Sound's Mosquito Fleet." HistoryLink.org Essay 869, 1999. Accessed Nov. 6, 2019. www.historylink.org/File/869.

Morgan, Murray. *The Last Wilderness.* Seattle: University of Washington Press, 1976.

"NOAA Designates New National Marine Sanctuary in Maryland." National Oce-anic and Atmospheric Administration, July 8, 2019. Accessed Nov. 3, 2019. www .noaa.gov/media-release/noaa-designates-new-national-marine-sanctuary -in-maryland.

"Report on the Timber Industry." Oregon Office of Economic Analysis, September 2018. Accessed Nov. 4, 2019. https://oregoneconomicanalysis.com/reports/.

Strochlic, Nina. " 'Ghost Fleet' of Sunken Warships Declared a National Marine Sanctuary." *National Geographic*, July 8, 2019. www.nationalgeographic.com /culture/2019/07/ghost-fleet-sunken-warships-declared-national-marine -sanctuary/.

US Census Bureau. "1880 Census, Vol. 8: Chapter VIII, Ship-Building Timber." Washington, DC.

Williams, David B. "Seattle Map 15—Mosquito Fleet 1908." *GeologyWriter.com* (blog), September 8, 2017. Accessed Nov. 6, 2019. http://geologywriter.com/tag /mosquito-fleet/.

Wright, E. W., ed. *Lewis and Dryden's Marine History of the Pacific Northwest*. Portland, OR: Lewis and Dryden, 1895.

Wright, Tim. "High-Lead Logging on the Olympic Peninsula 1920s–1930s." Center for the Study of the Pacific Northwest, University of Washington, Seattle, 2019. Accessed Nov. 6, 2019. www.washington.edu/uwired/outreach/cspn/Website /Classroom%20Materials/Curriculum%20Packets/High%20Lead%20Logging /High-Lead%20Logging%20Main.html.

CHAPTER 5

Ahlstrom, R. V. N., J. S. Dean, and W. J. Robinson. "Evaluating Tree-Ring Interpretations at Walpi Pueblo, Arizona." *American Antiquity* 56, no. 4 (1991): 628–644.

Anderton, L., D. McAvoy, and M. Kuhns. "Native American Uses of Utah Forest Trees." Utah State University Cooperative Extension, 2011. Accessed Nov. 3, 2019. https://digitalcommons.usu.edu/cgi/viewcontent .cgi?referer=&httpsredir=1&article=2211&context=extension_curall.

Asimov, Eric. "Clear Creek Eaux de Vie." *Diner's Journal* (blog). *New York Times*, August 15, 2007. https://dinersjournal.blogs.nytimes.com/2007/08/15 /clear-creek-eaux-de-vie.

Ault, Alicia. "Medicine Creek, the Treaty That Set the Stage for Standing Rock." *Smithsonian*, June 9, 2017. www.smithsonianmag.com/smithsonian-institution /standing-rock-there-was-medicine-creek-180963623.

Bernick, K. *Water Hazard (DgRs 30) Artifact Recovery Project Report*. Victoria, BC: British Columbia Archaeology Branch, 1989.

Betancourt, J. L., and T. R. Van Devender. "Holocene Vegetation in Chaco Canyon, New Mexico." *Science* 214 (1981): 656–658.

Bouchard, R., and D. I. D. Kennedy. "Utilization of Fishes, Beach Foods, and Marine Mammals by the Tl'uhus Indian People of British Columbia." British Columbia Indian Language Project, Victoria. Unpublished manuscript, 1974.

Captain Cook Society and I. Boreham, eds. "Resolution Cove, Bligh Island, British Columbia, Canada." Accessed Nov. 5, 2019. www.captaincooksociety.com/home /detail/resolution-cove-bligh-island-british-columbia-canada.

"Coast Douglas-Fir in the Laird's Grove, Ardentinny, Scotland, United Kingdom." Monumental Trees, 2016. Accessed Nov. 5, 2019. www.monumentaltrees.com /en/gbr/scotland/argyllandbute/14066_lairdsgrove/26989/.

Corder, S. E. "Properties and Uses of Bark as an Energy Source." Research Paper 31, Oregon State University, Corvallis, 1976.

Croes, Dale R. *The Hoko River Archaeological Site Complex: The Wet/Dry Site (45CA213), 3,000–1,700 B.P.* Pullman: Washington State University Press, 1995.

Crooks, D. W. "Governor Isaac I. Stevens and the Medicine Creek Treaty, Prelude to the War in Southern Puget Sound." *Pacific Northwest Forum* X (1985): 23–35.

Da Ronch, F., G. Caudullo, and D. de Rigo. "*Pseudotsuga menziesii* in Europe: Distribution, Habitat, Usage, and Threats." In European Atlas of Forest Tree Species, ed. J. San-Miguel-Ayanz, D. de Rigo, G. Caudullo, T. H. Durrant, and A. Mauri, 146–147. Luxembourg: Publications Office of the European Union, 2016.

Decker, Doug. "Tillamook Burn." The Oregon Encyclopedia. Oregon Historical Society, 2018. Accessed Nov. 3, 2019. https://oregonencyclopedia.org/articles /tillamook_burn/#.Wt0c9ojwZPY.

Gough, B. M. "Forests and Sea Power: A Vancouver Island Economy, 1778–1875." *Journal of Forest History* 32, no. 3 (1988): 117–124.

Green, Constance. "Douglas Fir or Spruce Tips: A Mighty Tree Enters the Kitchen." *The Wine Forest Blog*. Wine Forest Wild Foods, October 30, 2015. Accessed Nov. 5, 2019. https://wineforest.com/blogs/the-wine-forest-blog/74581700-douglas -fir-or-spruce-tips-a-mighty-tree-enters-the-kitchen.

Gunther, Erna. *Ethnobotany of Western Washington: The Knowledge and Use of Indigenous Plants by Native Americans*. Seattle: University of Washington Press, 1973.

Hall, J. A. *Utilization of Douglas-Fir Bark*. US Forest Service Pacific Northwest Forest and Range Experiment Station, Miscellaneous Report, 1971.

Hazard, Joseph T. *Medicine Creek Treaty: Companion to Adventure*. Portland, OR: Binfords and Mort, 1952.

Jones, Leslie. "First Spar for USS *Constitution*." Digital Commonwealth, 1929. Accessed Nov. 5, 2019. www.digitalcommonwealth.org/search /commonwealth:5t34sz50n.

Laferrière, J. E., and W. Van Asdall. "Plant Use in Mountain Pima Holiday Decorations." *Kiva* 57, no. 1 (1991): 27–38.

Lewis, James G. *The Forest Service and the Greatest Good: A Centennial History*. Durham, NC: Forest History Society, 2005.

Lightfoot, Ricky R. "Roofing an Early Anasazi Great Kiva: Analysis of an Architectural Model." *Kiva* 53, no. 3 (1988): 253–272.

MacMillan, H. R. "Timber Markets of India." *The Timbermen* 17 (1916): 33–34.

Mapes, Lynda V. "After 153 Years, Treaty Tree Lost to Winter Storm." *Seattle Times*, February 12, 2007. www.seattletimes.com/seattle-news /after-153-years-treaty-tree-lost-to-winter-storm.

Minor, R., and W. C. Grant. "Earthquake-Induced Subsidence and Burial of Late Holocene Archaeological Sites, Northern Oregon Coast." *American Antiquity* 61, no. 4 (1996): 772–781.

Moerman, Daniel E. *Native American Ethnobotany*. Portland, OR: Timber Press, 1998.

Nakai, Glynnis. "Nisqually National Wildlife Refuge History." US Fish and Wildlife Service, 2019. Accessed Nov. 5, 2019. www.fws.gov/refuges/profiles/History .cfm?ID=13529.

National Association of Railroad Tie Producers. "Tie Producers Discuss Production Outlook." *Railway Age* 68 (1920): 1295–1298.

Plywood Pioneers Association. *Plywood in Retrospect: Portland Manufacturing Company*. Tacoma, WA: Plywood Pioneers Association, 1967. www.apawood.org /data/Sites/1/documents/monographs/1-portland-manufacturing-co.pdf.

Robbins, W., J. Harrington, and B. Freire-Marreco. *Ethnobotany of the Tewa Indians*. Bureau of American Ethnology Bulletin 55. Washington, DC: Government Printing Office, 1916. 42–44.

Sekaquaptewa, E., and D. Washburn. "They Go Along Singing: Reconstructing the Hopi Past from Ritual Metaphors in Song and Image." *American Antiquity* 69, no. 3 (2004): 457–486.

Sharma, R. P. *The Indian Forester* 27 (1901): 573.

Shaw, J. D. "Economies of Driftwood: The Role of Extralocal Resources in Island Ecosystems." Presented at the Society for American Archaeology Annual Meeting, Vancouver, BC, 2008.

Steen, Harold K. *The U.S. Forest Service: A History*. Durham, NC: Forest History Society, 2004.

"Tallest Wooden Flagpole and Largest Flag." *Popular Mechanics* August 1914: 208.

Tucker, K. "Indians Fish at Willamette Falls." The Oregon History Project, Oregon Historical Society, 2003. Accessed Nov. 3, 2019. https://oregonhistoryproject.org/articles/historical-records/indians-fish-at-willamette-falls.

Turner, N.J., L.C. Thompson, M.T. Thompson, and A.Z. York. *Thompson Ethnobotany: Knowledge and Naming of Plants by the Thompson Indians of British Columbia*. Royal British Columbia Museum, Memoir No. 3. 1990.

Turner, N., and M. A. M. Bell. "The Ethnobotany of the Southern Kwakiutl Indians of British Columbia." *Economic Botany* 27 (1973): 257–310.

US Forest Service. "Charcoal Kilns Interpretive Site." Cariboo-Targhee National Forest, Special Places. Accessed Nov. 4, 2019. www.fs.usda.gov/recarea/ctnf/recarea/?recid=53861.

Varney, Philip. *Ghost Towns of the Mountain West: Your Guide to the Hidden History and Old West Haunts of Colorado, Wyoming, Idaho, Montana, Utah, and Nevada*. Beverly, MA: Voyageur Press, 2010.

World Monuments Fund. "Walpi Village." 2012. Accessed Nov. 5, 2019. www.wmf.org/project/walpi-village.

Wyoming State Historical Society. "Piedmont Charcoal Kilns." WyoHistory.org, 2019. Accessed Nov. 5, 2019. www.wyohistory.org/field-trips/piedmont-charcoal-kilns.

CHAPTER 6

Agee, James K. *Fire Ecology of Pacific Northwest Forests*. Washington, DC: Island Press, 1996.

Anderson, M. Kat. *Tending the Wild: Native American Knowledge and the Management of California's Natural Resources*. Berkeley: University of California Press, 2005.

Arno, S. F., and G. E. Gruell. "Douglas-Fir Encroachment into Mountain Grasslands in Southwestern Montana." *Journal of Range Management* 39, no. 3 (1986): 272–275.

Arno, S. F., J. H. Scott, and M. G. Hartwell. "Age-Class Structure of Old Growth Ponderosa Pine/Douglas-Fir Stands and Its Relation to Fire History." US Forest Service Intermountain Research Station, Research Paper INT-RP-481, 1995.

Boyd, Robert, ed. *Indians, Fire, and the Land in the Pacific Northwest*. Corvallis: Oregon State University Press, 1999.

Brown, P. M., and T. W. Swetnam. "A Cross-Dated Fire History from Coast Redwood near Redwood National Park, California." *Canadian Journal of Forest Research* 24, no. 1 (1994): 21–31.

DeLuca, T. H., M. D. MacKenzie, M. J. Gundale, and W. E. Holben. "Wildfire-Produced Charcoal Directly Influences Nitrogen Cycling in Ponderosa Pine Forests." *Soil Science Society of America Journal* 70, no. 2 (2006): 448–453. https://dl.sciencesocieties.org/publications/sssaj/abstracts/70/2/448.

Fiedler, C. E., P. Friederici, M. Petruncio, C. Denton, and W. D. Hacker. "Managing for Old Growth in Frequent-Fire Landscapes." *Ecology and Society* 12, no. 2 (2007): 1–12. Article 20.

Glickstein, D. "Twain's Great Northwest Tour." *Washington Magazine* 3, no. 4 (1986): 44–47.

Grissino-Mayer, H. D., C. M. Gentry, S. Croy, J. Hiatt, B. Osborne, A. Stan, and G. D. Wight. "Fire History of Western Montana Forested Landscapes via Tree-Ring Analyses." In Professional Paper 23, 47–56. Laboratory of Tree-Ring Science, University of Tennessee, Knoxville, 2006.

Gruell, G. E. "Fire and Vegetative Trends in the Northern Rockies: Interpretations from 1871–1982 Photographs." US Forest Service Intermountain Research Station, General Technical Report INT-GTR-158, 1983.

———. "Indian Fires in the Interior West: A Widespread Influence." In *Proceedings: Symposium and Workshop on Wilderness Fire*, 68–80. US Forest Service Intermountain Research Station, General Technical Report INT-GTR-182, 1985.

Heyerdahl, E. K., R. F. Miller, and R. A. Parsons. "History of Fire and Douglas-Fir Establishment in a Savanna and Sagebrush-Grassland Mosaic, Southwestern Montana, USA." *Forest Ecology and Management* 230 (2006): 107–118.

Houston, D. B. "Wildfires in Northern Yellowstone National Park." *Ecology* 54, no. 5 (1973): 1111–1117.

Levy, S. "Rekindling Native Fires." *BioScience* 55, no. 4 (2005): 303–308.

Meagher, M., and D. B. Houston. *Yellowstone and the Biology of Time: Photographs Across a Century*. Norman: University of Oklahoma Press, 1998.

Morrison, P. H., and F. J. Swanson. "Fire History and Pattern in a Cascade Range Landscape." US Forest Service Pacific Northwest Research Station, General Technical Report PNW-GTR-254, 1990.

Parker, T. J., K. M. Clancy, and R. L. Mathiasen. "Interactions among Fire, Insects and Pathogens in Coniferous Forests of the Interior Western United States and Canada." *Agricultural and Forest Entomology* 8 (2006): 167–189.

Pinchot, Gifford. *Breaking New Ground*. New York: Harcourt, Brace, 1947.

Taylor, A. H., and C. N. Skinner. "Fire History and Landscape Dynamics in a Late-Successional Reserve, Klamath Mountains, California, USA." *Forest Ecology and Management* 111 (1998): 285–301.

Thornton, William A. *Diary of William Anderson Thornton: Military Expedition to New Mexico*. 1855–1856. Electronic version produced by S. C. Blair and S. Stafford. The Kansas Collection. www.kancoll.org/articles/thornton.htm.

Wray, Jacilee, and M. Kat Anderson. "Restoring Indian-Set Fires to Prairie Ecosystems on the Olympic Peninsula." *Ecological Restoration* 21, no. 4 (2003): 296–301.

CHAPTER 7

Apostol, Dean, and Marcia Sinclair, eds. *Restoring the Pacific Northwest: The Art and Science of Ecological Restoration in Cascadia*. Washington, DC: Island Press, 2006.

Arno, S. F., J. H. Scott, and M. G. Hartwell. "Age-Class Structure of Old Growth Ponderosa Pine/Douglas-Fir Stands and Its Relation to Fire History." US Forest Service Intermountain Research Station, Research Paper INT-RP-481, 1995.

Arno, Stephen F., and Carl E. Fiedler. "Restoring Inland Northwest Forests: Ponderosa Pine and Interior Forests." In *Encyclopedia for Restoration of Pacific Northwest Ecosystems*, ed. Dean Apostol and Marcia Sinclair. Washington, DC: Island Press, 2006.

Arno, Stephen F., and Steven Allison-Bunnell. *Flames in Our Forest: Disaster or Renewal?* Washington, DC: Island Press, 2001.

Blankenbuehler, Paige. "Wildfires Don't Hurt Hot Real Estate Markets." *High Country News,* October 4, 2018. www.hcn.org/articles/wildfire-wildfires -dont-hurt-hot-real-estate-markets.

Brown, A., and K. P. Davis. *Forest Fire: Control and Use.* 2nd ed. New York: McGraw-Hill, 1973.

Cornwall, Warren. "Why Does This Famous Protector of Trees Now Want to Cut Some Down?" *Science* magazine, October 5, 2017. Accessed Nov. 6, 2019. www.sciencemag.org/news/2017/10/why-does-famous-protector-trees -now-want-cut-some-down.

Fiedler, Carl E. "Natural Process-Based Management of Fire-Adapted Western Forests." In *Proceedings of Small Diameter Timber: Resource Management, Manufacturing, and Markets.* Pullman: Washington State University Cooperative Extension, 2002.

Fiedler, C. E., K. L. Metlen, and E. K. Dodson. "Restoration Treatment Effects on Stand Structure, Tree Growth, and Fire Hazard in a Ponderosa Pine/Douglas-Fir Forest in Montana." *Forest Science* 56, no. 1 (2010): 18–31.

Fiedler, C. E., S. F. Arno, C. E. Keegan, and K. A. Blatner. "Overcoming America's Wood Deficit: An Overlooked Option." *BioScience* 51, no. 1 (2001): 53–58.

Fonda, R. W., and L. C. Bliss. "Forest Vegetation of the Montane and Subalpine Zones, Olympic Mountains, Washington." *Ecological Monographs* 39, no. 3 (1969): 271–301.

Franklin, J. F., D. R. Berg, D. A. Thornburgh, and J. C. Tappeiner. "Alternative Silvicultural Approaches to Timber Harvesting: Variable Retention Harvest Systems." In *Creating a Forestry for the 21st Century,* ed. K. A. Kohm and J. F. Franklin. Washington, DC: Island Press, 1997.

Franklin, J. F., K. N. Johnson, and D. L. Johnson. *Ecological Forest Management.* Long Grove, IL: Waveland Press, 2018.

Franklin, J. F., T. A. Spies, R. Van Pelt, A. B. Carey, D. A. Thornburgh, D. R. Berg, D. B. Lindenmayer, M. E. Harmon, W. S. Keeton, D. C. Shaw, K. Bible, and J. Chen. "Disturbances and Structural Development of Natural Forest Ecosystems with Silvicultural Implications, Using Douglas-Fir Forests as an Example." *Forest Ecology and Management* 155 (2002): 399–423.

Harrod, R. J., B. H. McRae, and W. E. Hartl. "Historical Stand Reconstruction in Ponderosa Pine Forests to Guide Silvicultural Prescriptions." *Forest Ecology and Management* 114 (1999): 433–446.

Kauffmann, Michael Edward. *Conifer Country: A Natural History and Hiking Guide to 35 Conifers of the Klamath Mountain Region.* Bayside, CA: Backcountry Press, 2012.

McCool, S. F., and G. H. Stankey. "Visitor Attitudes Toward Wilderness Fire Management Policy, 1971–84." US Forest Service Intermountain Research Station, Research Paper INT-RP-357, 1986.

Metlen, K. L., and C. E. Fiedler. "Restoration Treatment Effects on the Understory of Ponderosa Pine/Douglas-Fir Forests in Western Montana, USA." *Forest Ecology and Management* 222 (2006): 355–369.

"Olympic National Park Fire Management." National Park Service. Accessed Oct. 30, 2019. www.nps.gov/olym/learn/management/fire-management-1.htm.

Perlin, John. *A Forest Journey*. Woodstock, VT: Countryman Press, 2005.

Pinchot, Gifford. "The Relation of Forests and Forest Fires." *National Geographic* 10 (1899): 393–403.

Pyne, Stephen J. *Fire in America: A Cultural History of Wildland and Rural Fire*. Princeton, NJ: Princeton University Press, 1982.

Sillett, S. C., R. Van Pelt, J. Freund, J. Campbell-Spickler, A. Carroll, and R. Kramer. "Development and Dominance of Douglas-Fir in North American Rainforests." *Forest Ecology and Management* 429 (2018): 93–114.

Stephens, S. L., J. J. Moghaddas, C. Edminster, C. E. Fiedler, S. Haase, H. Harrington, J. E. Keeley, E. Knapp, J. D. McIver, K. Metlen, C. Skinner, and A. Youngblood. "Fire and Fire Surrogate Treatment Effects on Vegetation Structure, Fuels, and Potential Fire Behavior and Severity from Six Western United States Coniferous Forests." *Ecological Applications* 19 (2009): 305–320.

Sudworth, George Bishop. *Forest Trees of the Pacific Slope*. US Department of Agriculture, Forest Service. Washington, DC: Government Printing Office, 1908.

US Forest Service. "Toward Shared Stewardship Across Landscapes: An Outcome-Based Investment Strategy." 2018. Accessed Nov. 6, 2019. www.fs.usda.gov/sites/default/files/toward-shared-stewardship.pdf.

A VISITOR'S GUIDE TO NOTABLE DOUGLAS-FIRS

"A Treehouse Grows in British Columbia by George Dyson." Treehouse by Design, July 25, 2006. https://treehousebydesign.com/blog/2006/07/25/a-treehouse-grows-in-british-columbia-by-george-dyson/.

Arno, Stephen F. *Discovering Sierra Trees*. Yosemite National Park, CA: Yosemite Natural History Association, 1973.

Bell, Cathy. "The Beautiful Buildings of Our National Parks." Cathybell.org, September 21, 2012. Accessed Nov. 5, 2019. Extensive personal website no longer maintained since her death in 2017.

"Bristlecone Pines." Great Basin National Park. National Park Service, 2016. Accessed Nov. 6. 2019. www.nps.gov/grba/planyourvisit/identifying-bristlecone-pines.htm.

"Capilano Suspension Bridge Park." Tourism Vancouver. Accessed Nov. 6, 2019. www.tourismvancouver.com/listings/capilano-suspension-bridge-park/17604/.

Capilano Suspension Bridge Park. "Treetops Adventure." Accessed Nov. 5, 2019. www.capbridge.com/explore/treetops-adventure/.

Charlet, David Alan. *Atlas of Nevada Conifers: A Phytogeographic Reference*. Reno: University of Nevada Press, 1996.

Currey, Donald R. "An Ancient Bristlecone Pine Stand in Eastern Nevada." *Ecology* 46, no. 4 (1965): 564–566.

Farris, C. A. "Spatial and Temporal Validation of Fire-Scar Fire Histories." PhD dissertation, University of Arizona, 2009.

Goodall, Mary. *Oregon's Iron Dream*. Portland, OR: Binfords and Mort, 1958.

Griffin, J. R. "A New Douglas-Fir Locality in Southern California." *Forest Science* 10, no. 3 (1964): 317–319.

REFERENCES

Hawthorn, Tom. "Kayak Builder a Prophet from the Wilderness." *Globe and Mail*, May 22, 2012. www.theglobeandmail.com/news/british-columbia /kayak-builder-a-prophet-from-the-wilderness/article4198917/.

"Hiking—Navajo Loop Trail." Utah.com. Accessed Nov. 5, 2019. https://utah.com /hiking/bryce-canyon-national-park/navajo-loop-trail.

"Historical Significance of Century Trees: Link to Native Americans." In *Century Trees*. City of Lake Oswego, OR, February 2010. Accessed Nov. 6, 2019. www.ci .oswego.or.us/sites/default/files/fileattachments/publicaffairs/web page/13678/century_tree_february_2010.pdf.

Hudson, C. S., and S. F. Sherwood. "The Occurrence of Melezitose in a Manna from the Douglas-Fir." *Journal of the American Chemical Society* 40, no. 9 (1918): 1456–1460.

Johnson, Charles G., Jr. *Alpine and Subalpine Vegetation of the Wallowa, Seven Devils, and Blue Mountains*. US Forest Service Pacific Northwest Region, 2004, 168–175.

Johnson, Peter. *Quarantined: Life and Death at William Head Station, 1872–1959*. Victoria, BC: Heritage House, 2013.

Josefsson, T., E. Sutherland, S. Arno, and L. östlund. "Ancient Bark-Peeled Trees in the Bitterroot Mountains, Montana: Legacies of Native Land Use and Implications for Their Protection." *Natural Areas Journal* 32 (2012): 54–64.

Krueger, Guenther. "The Lepers of Bentinck." *The Beaver* 69 (1989): 60–62.

Lee, Brian. "Forty Years Past: The Voyage of the *Orenda II*." *Harbour Spiel*, December 2018, 16–21.

———. "Forty Years Past: The Voyage of the *Orenda II* (Part 2)." *Harbour Spiel*, January 2019, 12–17.

Mathews, D., and P. Cady. "Douglas-Fir Culturally Modified Trees: Some Initial Considerations." Paper presented at the Northwest Anthropological Conference, Victoria, British Columbia, 2008.

Osler, Sanford. *Canoe Crossings: Understanding the Craft That Helped Shape British Columbia*. Victoria, BC: Heritage House, 2014.

"Peg Tree." Oregon Travel Information Council, September 24, 2011. Accessed Nov. 5, 2019. http://oregontic.com/oregon-heritage-trees/peg-tree/.

"Restoring the Historic Glacier Park Lodge." Glacier Park Collection. 2019. Accessed Nov. 6, 2019. www.glacierparkcollection.com/lodging/glacier-park-lodge /stories/restoration-at-glacier-park-lodge/.

Rodebaugh, Dale. "State Champion: Douglas Fir North of Town Is Colo.'s Tallest." *Durango Herald*, July 25, 2014.

Stall, Robert. "A Man, a Tree, and an Ocean to Cross." *Maclean's*, March 5, 1979, 4–5, 8.

Stewart, Hilary. *Cedar: Tree of Life to the Northwest Coast Indians*. Seattle: University of Washington Press, 1984.

"Sugar from the Douglas Fir." *Scientific American* 122 (1920): 165, 174–175.

INDEX

ABOUT THE AUTHORS

Bonnie Arno

STEPHEN F. ARNO (left) holds a PhD in forestry and plant science and is retired from a career as a research forester with the US Forest Service. Since 1973, he has authored or coauthored six books about forests and trees, including two Mountaineers Books titles, *Northwest Trees* and *Timberline*. **CARL E. FIEDLER** (right) has a PhD in forestry and ecology and is a retired professor from the University of Montana. Steve and Carl have coauthored two previous books together, most recently *Ponderosa: People, Fire, and the West's Most Iconic Tree*. Both Carl and Steve reside in Missoula, Montana.

recreation · lifestyle · conservation

MOUNTAINEERS BOOKS, including its two imprints, Skipstone and Braided River, is a leading publisher of quality outdoor recreation, sustainability, and conservation titles. As a 501(c)(3) nonprofit, we are committed to supporting the environmental and educational goals of our organization by providing expert information on human-powered adventure, sustainable practices at home and on the trail, and preservation of wilderness.

Our publications are made possible through the generosity of donors, and through sales of 700 titles on outdoor recreation, sustainable lifestyle, and conservation. To donate, purchase books, or learn more, visit us online:

MOUNTAINEERS BOOKS

1001 SW Klickitat Way, Suite 201 • Seattle, WA 98134
800-553-4453 • mbooks@mountaineersbooks.org • www.mountaineersbooks.org

An independent nonprofit publisher since 1960

 Mountaineers Books is proud to support the Leave No Trace Center for Outdoor Ethics, whose mission is to promote and inspire responsible outdoor recreation through education, research, and partnerships. The Leave No Trace program is focused specifically on human-powered (nonmotorized) recreation. For more information, visit www.lnt.org.

YOU MAY ALSO LIKE